A RABBI TALKS WITH JESUS

A Rabbi
Talks
with Jesus

Revised Edition

JACOB NEUSNER

McGill-Queen's University Press
Montreal & Kingston · London · Chicago

© McGill-Queen's University Press 2000
ISBN 978-0-7735-2046-2 (paper)
ISBN 978-0-7735-6839-6 (ePDF)

Legal deposit second quarter 2000
Bibliothèque nationale du Québec

Printed in Canada on acid-free paper that is 100% ancient forest free
(100% post-consumer recycled), processed chlorine free
Reprinted 2001, 2007, 2012, 2015

This is a revised and expanded version of *A Rabbi Talks with Jesus: An Intermillennial, Interfaith Exchange,* published by Doubleday in 1993.

McGill-Queen's University Press acknowledges the support of the Canada
Council for the Arts for our publishing program. We also acknowledge the
financial support of the Government of Canada through the Canada Book
Fund for our publishing activities.

Canadian Cataloguing in Publication Data

Neusner, Jacob, 1932 –
 A rabbi talks with Jesus
 Originally published: New York: Doubleday, c1993.
 ISBN 978-0-7735-2046-2 (paper)
 ISBN 978-0-7735-6839-6 (ePDF)
 1. Jesus Christ – Jewish interpretations. I. Title.
 BM620.N48 2000   232.9'06   C99-901318-1

This book was typeset by Interscript in 10/12 Palatino.

IN MEMORY OF

Jerry Donald "Rip" Strange
Tyler, Texas

FATHER OF MY FRIEND AND COLLEAGUE
James F. Strange

Contents

CONTENTS

Acknowledgments

Grateful acknowledgment is made to the Max Richter Foundation for financial support. I am grateful for help and counsel to Stuart Silverman, William Scott Green, Laurence Tisch, and to my colleagues in the Department of Religious Studies, the University of South Florida.

For the most part, translations of scriptural verses are from *The Holy Bible. Revised Standard Version* (New York: Thomas Nelson & Sons, 1952), Old Testament Section, copyright 1952, New Testament Section, copyright 1946, by Division of Christian Education of the National Council of the Churches of Christ in the United States of America, by permission.

Foreword

This book is destined to be a minor classic and here minor is not a dismissive term. There are in world culture not many classics and few that are major, so even in our age of rhetorical inflation, "minor classic" is high praise.

A Rabbi Talks with Jesus is a revised and expanded version of a volume that appeared fairly recently (1993) and disappeared quickly, though not before attracting some fervent admirers. A large part of the problem with the original edition was that the U.S. publisher appended a rebarbative subtitle on the otherwise lively work – "an intermillennial exchange" – and this repelled all but the most determined book buyers.

Rabbi Jacob Neusner's volume is an example of a genre that we have seen only rarely since the High Middle Ages. The work harkens back to those few brief moments when the most learned men in the western world – medieval Rabbis, informed by Arabic learning, and Christian Schoolmen, particularly Thomists – conducted civil and honest debates with each other about the nature of God's One Truth. Those rare moments of respectful and erudite encounter flicker in the past's long blackness of intolerance and intentional misunderstanding.

Professor Neusner reanimates the ancient form and does so with an amiability that is contagious. I imagine that many Christians and Jews will wish to argue with him; but I also expect that they will wish to do so with the same mixture of friendliness and respect for the other person's faith that he so clearly evinces.

This classic form of Jewish-Christian encounter bypasses a particularly unattractive form of mutual engagement that has become especially shrill in recent years: the battle joined as a result of some Christian sects' attempt to proselytize members of the Jewish community through the presentation of Yeshua of Nazareth as a Jewish figure whom one can embrace as Moshiah and do so while continuing to be a practising Jew. Such present-day battles, fought with venom on both sides, inevitably are conducted on Christian terms. The Jewish defenders are placed in the position of having to deal with a Christian-defined articulation of the characteristics of Moshiah and then of having to argue that Yeshua of Nazareth did not fill that job description.

Rabbi Neusner's gentle discussion avoids both the intellectual sterility and the acrimony of such engagements. He simply presents a case that the Jesus who is depicted in the Christian scriptures – he uses the Gospel of St Matthew as his text – did not understand Torah very well. This procedure elegantly elides the question of whether or not the historical Jesus (the "real" figure behind Jesus-the-Christ, as found in the Gospels) made these same errors. Instead, it leads ineluctably to an inference that all believers, Christians and Jews alike, should ponder: that the Jewish and the Christian faiths really are distinct entities, operating on different premises and incapable of being melded together, save through indifference or ignorance. And thus, a friendly and respectful definition of irreducible difference is a mitzvah or, perhaps, a work of supererogation.

Donald Harman Akenson

A RABBI TALKS WITH JESUS

1

Come, Let Us Reason Together

I n this book I explain in a very straightforward and unapologetic way why, if I had been in the Land of Israel in the first century, I would not have joined the circle of Jesus's disciples. I would have dissented, I hope courteously, I am sure with solid reason and argument and fact. If I heard what he said in the Sermon on the Mount, for good and substantive reasons I would not have followed him.

That may be hard for people to imagine, since it is difficult to think of words more deeply etched into our civilization and its deepest affirmations than the teachings of the Sermon on the Mount and other teachings of Jesus. But then it also is hard to imagine hearing those words for the first time, as something surprising and demanding, not as mere clichés of culture. That is precisely what I propose to do here: listen and argue.

I write this book to shed some light on why, while Christians believe in Jesus Christ and the good news of his rule in the kingdom of Heaven, Jews believe in the Torah of Moses and form on earth and in their own flesh God's kingdom of priests and the holy people. And that belief requires faithful Jews to enter a dissent at the teachings of Jesus, on the grounds that those teachings at important points contradict the Torah.

Where Jesus diverges from the revelation by God to Moses at Mount Sinai, he is wrong, and Moses is right. In setting forth the grounds to this unapologetic dissent, I mean to foster religious dialogue among believers, Christian and Jewish alike. For a long time, Jews have praised Jesus as a rabbi, a Jew like us really; but to Christian faith in Jesus Christ, that affirmation is monumentally irrelevant. And for their part, Christians have praised Judaism as the religion from which Jesus came, and to us, that is hardly a compliment.

Jews and Christians have avoided meeting head-on the points of substantial difference between us, not only in response to the person and claims of Jesus, but especially in addressing his teachings. He claimed to reform and to improve, "You have heard it said ... but I say ..." *We Jews maintain, and I argue here, that the Torah was and is perfect and beyond improvement, and that Judaism built upon the Torah and the prophets and writings, the originally oral parts of the Torah written down in the Mishnah, Talmuds, and Midrash – that Judaism was and remains God's will for humanity.* By that criteria I propose to set forth a Jewish dissent to some important teachings of Jesus. It is a gesture of respect for Christians and honor for their faith. For we can argue only if we take one another seriously. But we can enter into dialogue only if we honor both ourselves and the other. In these pages I treat Jesus with respect, but I also mean to argue with him about things he says.

What's at stake here? If I succeed, Christians will find renewal for their faith in Jesus Christ – but also respect for Judaism. I mean to explain to Christians why I believe in Judaism, and that ought to help Christians identify the critical convictions that bring them to church every Sunday. Jews will strengthen their commitment to the Torah of Moses – but also respect for Christianity. I want Jews to understand why Judaism demands assent – "the All-Merciful

COME, LET US REASON TOGETHER

seeks the heart," "the Torah was given only to purify the human heart." Each party will locate here the very points on which the difference between Judaism and Christianity rests.

What makes me so certain of that outcome? Because I believe, when each side understands in the same way the issues that divide the two, and both with solid reason affirm their respective truths, then all may love and worship God in peace – knowing that it really is the one and the same God whom together they serve – in difference. So this is a religious book about religious difference: an argument about God.

My goal is to help Christians become better Christians, because they may come in these pages to a clearer account of what they affirm in their faith; and to help Jews become better Jews, because they will realize here – so I hope – that God's Torah is the way (not only our way, but the way) to love and serve the one God, creator of heaven and earth, who called us to serve and sanctify God's Name. *My point is simple. By the truth of the Torah, much that Jesus said is wrong.* By the criterion of the Torah, Israel's religion in the time of Jesus was authentic and faithful, not requiring reform or renewal, demanding only faith and loyalty to God and the sanctification of life through carrying out God's will.

Do I then propose that, after they have read my book, Christians reexamine their convictions about Christianity? Not at all. Christian faith finds a legion of reasons for believing in Jesus Christ (not merely that Jesus was and is Christ); all I argue is, maybe so, but not because he fulfilled the Torah or sustained the Torah or conformed to the Torah; not because he improved on the Torah. But, of course, Christian faith has never found troubling the fact of its own autonomy: not a mere continuation and reform of the prior faith, Judaism (always represented as corrupt and venal and hopeless anyhow), but a new beginning. So this argument – set forth on a level playing field – should not trouble the faithful. And I don't mean it to. But if Christians take seriously the claim that the criterion of Matthew is valid – not to destroy

5

but to fulfill – then I do think Christians may well have to reconsider the Torah ("Judaism" in secular language): Sinai calls, the Torah tells us how God wants us to be.

Do I mean, then, to set forth an argument of Jewish apologetics that consists in the rather tired claim, yes to the historical Jesus, no to the Christ of Christianity? For not a few apologists for Judaism (including Christian apologists for Judaism) distinguish between the Jesus who lived and taught, whom they honor and revere, from the Christ whom the Church (so they say) invented. They will maintain that the apostle, Paul, invented Christianity; Jesus, for his part, taught only truth, which, as believers in Judaism, we can affirm. In these pages I take a different path altogether. I am not interested in what happened later on; I want to know, how, if I were there, standing at the foot of the mountain where Jesus said the words that came to be called "the Sermon on the Mount," I would have responded.

So my dissent is entered not against "Christianity" in all its forms and versions, nor is it against the apostle, Paul, nor even against that complex and enormous "body of Christ" that the Church was and would become. And I mean to offer no apology for a "Judaism" that focuses upon that negative "Why not Christ?" Judaism does not have always to explain "why not," when the message of the Torah is always: Why ... because ... Judaism in all its complex forms constitutes something other than merely Christianity without Christ (the Old Testament without the New, in terms of revealed writings). Judaism is simply another religion, not merely not-Christianity; and at issue here is not Judaism as against Christianity or Jesus as against Christ (in that formulation in narrowly biographical-historical terms, which I find irrelevant to argument).

This is not a book about scholarship. I address only one picture of what Jesus said, that of the Gospel according to Matthew. For reasons spelled out in the discussion following, I have chosen that Gospel as particularly appropriate for the dialogue with the

Torah, or Judaism. The Jesus with whom I compose my argument is not the historical Jesus of a scholar's studious imagination, and that is for a simple reason: those fabricated historical figures are too many and diverse for an argument. Moreover, I don't see how religious people can differ about what confronts them only in scholarly works. When Jews open the New Testament, they assume they are hearing from the Jesus Christ of Christianity, and when Christians open the same book, they surely take the same view. That is not to say the historical Jesus is not a presence within and behind the Gospels; it is only to affirm that the Gospels as we read them portray Jesus to most of us who propose to know him. I write for believing Christians and faithful Jews; for them, Jesus is known through the Gospels. I address one of those Gospels.

Since we have out of the first century a variety of pictures of Jesus, who he was, what he said and did, and why he matters, let me explain why I chose Matthew's Jesus with which to conduct my debate. I decided to argue with that particular Jesus – that is, the picture of Jesus Christ set forth in the Gospel of St. Matthew (to use Christian language) – because by common consensus, Matthew's is the most "Jewish" of the Gospels, with its stress on issues of special interest to the Torah and to the people, Israel, to whom Jesus spoke.

Matthew speaks to us in particular. For we, Israel, are the ones to whom the issue of the Torah takes precedence, the ones for whom the statement resonates, *"Think not that I have come to abolish the Torah and the prophets; I have come not to abolish them but to fulfil them. For truly I say to you, till heaven and earth pass away, not an iota, not a dot, will pass from the Torah until all is accomplished. Whoever then relaxes one of the least of these commandments and teaches men so, shall be called least in the kingdom of heaven; but he who does them and teaches them shall be called great in the kingdom of heaven."* Out of Judaism, to this I say, "Amen, brother." So do I believe, too, just like you, with all my heart and soul and might.

7

Matthew's Jesus comes closest to an account of Jesus that a believing and practicing Jew can grasp in terms of Judaism. And
Matthew's picture of Jesus describes him as a Jew among Jews,
an Israelite at home in Israel, unlike the portrait, for instance,
given by John, who speaks of "the Jews" with hatred.
What makes an argument plausible and why now in particular? An argument with Matthew's Jesus is plausible because
there really is a shared Torah between us, so we can agree suffi-
ciently on the main thing to disagree on other things. By contrast,
there is a very good reason that I cannot argue with John's Jesus
or Luke's Jesus or Mark's Jesus. John and therefore his Jesus simply loathes "the Jews" – and enough said. Mark's and Luke's
Jesus, sharing much to be sure with Matthew, do not represent
figures for whom the Judaic connection nourishes.
Written probably in the last third of the first century, somewhere
outside of the Land of Israel, the Gospel according to St. Matthew,
deriving from a school or church whose writings came forth under
the name of Matthew, tells about chapters in the life, teachings and
miracles, death and resurrection of Jesus of Nazareth. Among
these matters, one is striking: the representation of Jesus as a
teacher, with an important message forming part of the evidence
that here is the Christ, in whom Israel should believe.
More to the point, the content of the message, not only the
character of the life and miracles, forms an important component
of Jesus' credentials in Matthew (but not, for example, in Paul's
letters). For Matthew, what Jesus said forms part of the testimony
to his claim. We – eternal Israel, to whom Jesus was sent by God
and to whom Jesus brought his message – are supposed to be
persuaded by the character of these teachings, represented as the
fulfillment of the Torah as a matter of fact. Accordingly, among
the many re-presentations of the figure of Jesus Christ, this story
laid heavy emphasis upon not only the death and resurrection of
Jesus Christ, but also upon his doings and sayings: miracles, instruction, parables.

Matthew claims in behalf of Jesus that his is a body of teachings of such obvious truth that all who hear them must confess the name of the one who said them: Jesus Christ. If these teachings in the mind of Matthew's Jesus do not form a central part of what Jesus stands for, then why tell us what he said, not only what he did, and what God did with him. If, after all, that is not the Evangelist's claim, then from the perspective of faith, no compelling reason required writing down so rich an account of the master's message. In response to the message of Matthew's Jesus, a practicing Jew such as myself, speaking for myself alone of course, but well within the faith of eternal Israel, can frame an argument.

Now, why with sayings but not with stories? If someone makes a categorical statement to do this, not that, you can argue. But how do you argue with a miracle? Either you believe or you do not believe. True, if you believe, you also draw the consequences that the faith wants you to draw, or you draw some other consequences. But, then the miracles are relevant only on the other side of conversion. Nor would any humane person, and certainly no Jew, child of a tradition that teaches God prefers the pursued to the pursuer – the lamb, the sheep, the goat, not the lion or the bear – wish to take issue with the tragic and disturbing Passion Narrative.

Nor can I conceive of an argument with a mother's tears or an empty tomb. And even among the sayings attributed by Matthew to Jesus, there is much in Matthew's story of Jesus that simply reviews well-known teachings of the Torah of Moses, for example, Jesus' well-known paraphrase of Leviticus 19: 18: "Love your neighbor as yourself." With that and much else that is good Torah-teaching, no faithful Jew would want to argue. But much set forth in fulfillment of the Torah in fact either violates the clear teaching and intent of the Torah, or offers a religious message inferior to that of the Torah as Israel reads the Torah. And an argument on that set of teachings to which judgments such as these pertain is precisely what I offer in these pages.

9

So it seems to me that a dialogue between Judaism and Christianity best begins with Matthew's Gospel, even though I make no claim whatsoever about the historical veracity of what Matthew says Jesus said and did. That is an issue confronting scholars. But I write as a religious Jew for believing Christians, and what I take to be Christian faith encompasses Matthew's account of Jesus. So the Christians with whom I mean to conduct a conversation are not only those who, calling themselves "Bible-believing" and called by others "fundamentalists," believe every word as written, but every Christian who finds Jesus (also) in Matthew's Gospel. Out there are millions and millions of Christians who really do find Jesus in Matthew's Gospel, and who will be willing to listen to a Jew's argument with the Jesus of Matthew's Gospel, an argument about the fundamental truths of the Torah and of Christ, as we shall see.

I insist then that we meet Matthew's Jesus on his own ground, taking as fact that he said the things that Matthew said he said: I take this Gospel seriously. To appreciate this effort of mine at religious dialogue, in a religious spirit, on religious issues, scholarly or theological readers, with their own conceptions of what Jesus really said or did, will have to suspend doubt. Everyone else, I hope, will go forward with me. Now to the matter at hand: Why take the Gospels seriously for the purpose of religious dialogue?

When religious people in mosques, synagogues, and churches take up the writings of their respective faiths, they find there what God has told to Muhammed or Moses or Jesus, true and factual stories about what the founders of Islam, Judaism, or Christianity have said and done. When scholars of Islam or Judaism or Christianity read these same writings, a fair number of them receive these writings not as God's word but as statements of what humanity has written down in God's name. In the case of the Gospels, therefore, the body of the faithful in the churches read words they assume Jesus said, accounts of what he did, while scholars in universities and in Christian seminaries alike find in

COME, LET US REASON TOGETHER

the Gospels evidence that – properly interpreted – may tell us about things Jesus "really" did or said. It follows that there is a considerable difference between how the faithful receive Scripture – as the word of God – and how scholars read this same Scripture – as (mere) evidence about what may or may not have been said.

That difference matters when we propose to address the claims of the faith and even conduct an argument about their truth. The Christian believer points to the man and what he said: here he is, here is the good news about him. Then the other, proposing to take seriously Christian faith in its own terms, may compose a response: here is what I want to say in response to who he is and what he said.

But how are we to argue not with the Gospels' Jesus but with the scholars' formulation of the man, his life and teachings? The range of scholarly opinion being diverse, the first challenge is to identify the Jesus with whom we are supposed to argue. The second is to negotiate the distinction, important to scholars but not to most believers, between the Jesus of history (that is, the scholars' formulation) and the Christ of faith (that is, everything else). At that point, when we turn away from a Gospel's account of Jesus Christ and direct attention toward historians' pictures of what, among the Gospels' accounts, we are supposed to address as what Jesus really said and did, we abandon the faithful altogether. We argue with someone else's Jesus rather than the Jesus of the Christians who find in the Gospels the person of Jesus Christ, God incarnate. At that point, how are religious people – Muslims or Christians or Jews – to compose a coherent argument among themselves? Coming with faith in one religion, a believer finds it necessary to confront not the faith of the faithful but the composite account fabricated on premises quite other than those of religious belief.

Now, when an outsider to Christianity proposes, as I do in this book, to compose an argument with Jesus, I face a choice: With which Jesus? Is it the one the scholars (this morning) tell me really lived and worked, said this (but not that), did this (but not the other thing)? Or the one Christian believers believe is son of God, who taught and did wonders, was tried by the Sanhedrin and sentenced by Pontius Pilate and crucified by the Romans and rose from the dead and sits at the right hand of God? Framing the question in that way, the answer is self-evident.

But in explaining why I propose to conduct a religious dialogue on the foundations of one of the Gospels instead of scholars' accounts of the historical Jesus, I have moved well ahead of my story. Let me start back with a simple statement of what is at stake in this work of religious argument, one which, if my goal is achieved, will make Christians better Christians, Jews better Jews, and sharpen the lines of difference – so opening a new path of religious dialogue for an irenic future.

It remains to answer a second question. Why did I write this book? Because I like Christians and respect Christianity and wanted to take seriously the faith of people I value. I cannot imagine a Jew who grew up in a Muslim country writing such a book about Muhammed (or surviving its publication for very long). But life in a Christian country, among Catholic and Protestants and Orthodox Christians alike, has made me proud of Judaism and happy to be what I am – but also glad to have as friends and neighbors a religion (among those I have known, at any rate) that fosters goodwill for the other, on the one side, and a genuine interest in good relations with those who differ, on the other.

Let me pay my tribute to those who modeled their lives on the teachings of Jesus, or tried to, or meant to. I grew up in West Hartford, Connecticut, a Reform Jew in a mainly Protestant suburb. In kindergarten, there were perhaps three other Jews, among about thirty; not a great many more Catholics; and of course no blacks at that time. What I remember in growing up in a time in which I celebrated Christmas in school and Hanukkah at home was that my Christian friends welcomed me into their world and respected mine. True, it was a shock to discover, in third grade, that the Pilgrims – we were drawing pictures for Thanksgiving – were not going to synagogue but to church, and I could not persuade Miss Melcher that they really went to the same Temple I did on Farmington Avenue.

But I also remember how Mrs. O'Brien, my best friend Billy's mother, wanted to give me crackers on Passover, because she knew that we Jews weren't eating bread that week. I remember how my sister was nearly always the Virgin Mary in our tableaus – the teachers wanted to be sure we felt at home. But I also recall how, in seventh grade, for the first time, our school celebrated Hanukkah as well as Christmas. And West Hartford believed it had progressed that year, and so did I. In all, in the world I remember, Christianity was benign and friendly and welcoming; Judaism was home, to be sure, but I never knew, then or later, that fearful face that Christianity in other times, or other places even in my own time, showed to the world. I grew up in a world that, as I remember it, was one of good will.

Since in these same years, millions of Jews were being murdered in Europe, and Jew-hatred flourished throughout the world, including my own state and town, I do not take for granted the fundamentally normal way in which I experienced the difference of being Jewish in a mostly Protestant world. It is a world that I respect and admire, in which I see virtue.

Not only so, but my life and calling, as a scholar of Judaism within the academic world of the study of religion, came about because Protestants and Catholics wanted Judaism in the academy and opened the way for a person of my commitments and vocation to teach. My ideal of studying Judaism within the mainstream of the academy formed in response to my teachers, then colleagues, who wanted me and the things I valued to be with them, in that center and heart of public learning. For example, I always wanted to become a rabbi (as it happens because of my upbringing, a Reform rabbi). When at Harvard college I explained to a selection board for a Henry Fellowship that I wanted to study at Oxford University to improve my knowledge of Jewish history, they sent me off for a year. When, later on, I explained to the selection board for a Kent Fellowship of the National Council for Religion in Higher Education, a creation of a professor at the Yale University Divinity School (Charles Foster Kent), that I wanted to go to graduate school to study for a Ph.D. in religion and to specialize in the study of Judaism, they gave me a generous fellowship and sent me on my way. That is the story of my life: "for that [the Torah] will be your wisdom and your understanding in the sight of the peoples" (Deut 4:6).

When I turned to Columbia University and Union Theological Seminary for doctoral studies, I was welcomed and given every courtesy and opportunity. When my degree was completed, John Hutcheson, then chairman at Columbia, invited me to join the faculty. Some years later, Fred Berthold of Dartmouth College did the same. And in the recent past, Frank Borkowski, a Roman Catholic president of a state university, who opens luncheons with a simple prayer that everyone joins and no one finds embarrassing, and some Methodist and Southern Baptist professors all joined together to bring me to, and receive me at, the University of South Florida, where I have found my place.

So my entire life and career from that time to this has been in the mainstream of American intellectual life, and if I have made my contribution in bringing Judaic learning into the mainstream, that has formed my highest ambition. The reason was, and is, that I value the life of my country and I want to contribute what I most prize to it, and I perceive that that contribution is wanted and welcome. My closest colleagues in my good years at Dartmouth College and now at the University of South Florida have been faithful Christians, who exhibit enormous esteem for Judaism. My publishers are many and varied, and I thank them all; but among them, the Christian academic presses – Trinity Press

COME, LET US REASON TOGETHER

International, Augsburg-Fortress, Westminster-John Knox, and Abingdon – have a special place in my heart. For they take enormous pride in giving a hearing to books of Judaism. That is the spirit in which I have given thought to this book and its companions: to give something back. Catholic and Protestant Christianity alike have brought forward, in my life, people whose religious convictions have led them to respect my religion, and to want to know more about it. Can I pay back anything less than a reasonable interest in their religion and an effort to join issue with it?

Since I am, so I believe, one of the earliest scholars in the study of Judaism, of Jewish origin and rabbinical education, to make a career entirely under secular auspices and never on a Jewish payroll of any kind (beyond my rabbinical studies), I can be understood when I say that the attitudes of this book respond to the experiences of a long life, nearing the age of sixty-eight as I write these words, within the academic and religious worlds of mainstream America, which is Christian. No wonder, then, that I have formed a respectful opinion of Christianity; but no wonder, too, that I have wanted to spell out in a reasonable way precisely where I think Christianity, beginning with Jesus (as portrayed in one Gospel), took a wrong turn in abandoning the Torah.

Well, then, what happens if this book succeeds, that is, if the dialogue between Judaism and Christianity becomes substantive, addressed to issues of truth and falsity, right and wrong, in the service of God? What is at stake is a first step in establishing a discourse of autonomy for Judaism. For a long time, in the discourse of Judaism and Christianity, Judaism has joined issue to defend itself, but not since the Middle Ages have Judaic parties to the dialogue addressed the convictions of Christianity in their own terms, or for that matter, set forth the convictions of Judaism in our own terms. In the autonomous framework of this book, I mean to say not only why I am not a Christian, but also why I think Christians should take seriously the claims of Sinai in shaping their Christianity. True, this is no work of proselytism. I didn't write this book to persuade Christian readers to leave the church and enter the synagogue. This is not Judaic tract, like the many obnoxious Christian tracts asking me to convert to Christianity that come in the mail day by day.

But this book does mean to present a challenge to Christian faith, setting forth the issues that seem to me to divide Christianity from Judaism in particular, and any such challenge contains within itself also an invitation to respond. I hope and believe that Christians will respond with a heartfelt reaffirmation of the faith, knowing what the issues are; if I make Christian life a firm decision, not merely a habit, I think I will have served a good cause.

And the same, obviously, is so for my fellow Jews. For those who imagine a secular existence for eternal Israel, I offer only life with God whom we know in and through the Torah. I think it is time to set forth a free-standing, and autonomous, mode of religious discourse for ourselves, in our American language and context, in which we explain ourselves to ourselves, without the intervention of our religious circumstance, however benign, of being a Judaic minority in a Christian world. I do not commence this labor of forming a discourse of autonomy for Judaism, far from it. I have the sense that the great European Jewish theologians and philosophers of our own century were moving in the direction that I take in these pages, toward an argument, on Judaic religious terms, with Christianity on its religious terms. Martin Buber's wonderful work, *Two Types of Faith*, is one example among many of an account that is far superior to any that I can set forth. Had European Judaism survived (and apart from some flowing wells of Orthodoxy, both segregationist and integrationist, Judaism is today a dead religion in Europe), the great intellects would have achieved that discourse of autonomy for Judaism that, in a simple and preliminary way, I aim to adumbrate here. I have been called a "Holocaust theologian," an honor I have not claimed for myself or earned. My life has been what it

has been because I am one who was left to do the work, not in response to the Holocaust, but in the aftermath of the Holocaust.
Better minds than mine thought about these things. I can only do
my best. As always, we live out our lives in the presence of the
ages. When it is our turn, we do our best. Then we hand on the
task to those who come after us. It is what it means to be one in
eternal Israel.

2

A Practicing Jew
in Dialogue with Jesus

*And he went about all Galilee, teaching in their synagogues and preaching
the gospel of the kingdom and healing every disease and every infirmity
among the people ... And great crowds followed him from Galilee and the
Decapolis and Jerusalem and Judea and from beyond the Jordan. Seeing the
crowds, he went up on the mountain, and when he sat down his disciples
came to him. And he opened his mouth and taught them, saying ...*

Matthew 4:23, 25; 5: 1–2

I magine walking on a dusty road in Galilee some summer,
meeting up with a small band of youngsters, led by a young
man. The man's presence catches your attention: he talks, the
others listen, respond, argue, obey – care what he says, follow
him. You don't know who the man is, but you do know he makes
a difference to the people with him and to nearly everybody he
meets. People respond, some with anger, some with admiration,
a few with genuine faith. But no one walks away uninterested in
the man and the things he says and does.

Now if you can make the leap over two thousand years, try to imagine that you have never heard of Christianity. All you know is a few sentences said by the man, a few stories told about him, some of the stories he told, some of the things he did. Can you come back to Galilee, to a meeting with Jesus before he went up to Jerusalem? Can you listen to words repeated countless times, as though these words were said for the very first time? Then, but only then, you can meet the man, with his disciples, and address the issue in the humble and immediate world in which you live: if you were there, what would you have done? If you didn't know what he would become (speaking now from the perspective of a faithful Christian), would you have adopted him as your master and followed him?

I think we can read the words that Matthew quotes in Jesus' name if, by an act of imagination, we can place ourselves on a dusty Galilean road and pretend, for a moment, that we have never before heard words that for centuries have echoed. Then, and only then, finding fresh and challenging what the centuries have made stale, we may renew the encounter – the meeting, the argument, the confrontation – that I think stands at the beginning of Christianity: the encounter with Jesus.

Today, with so many teachings turned into platitudes and clichés, it is difficult to hear his words as challenges, goads, assertions in the face of contrary views. But that is our task, too, if we are to have a serious argument about important truths. And it is time, I think, for some specific teachings of Matthew's Jesus to receive sustained and serious attention as not platitudes and truisms but contentious and vigorous propositions, demanding assent attained through argument. For, as you read the stories Matthew tells, you cannot avoid the simple fact that Jesus was a man who said things he thought new and important, and who claimed that his teachings formed the correct way to carry out and to fulfill the Torah, the teachings that God had given to Moses at Mount Sinai.

What honor accrues if Christians take as gospel-truth, and Jews pretend to ignore, allegations about what God wants of us that Jesus put forth? These he meant as argument, in criticism of the views of others, and that he taught as powerful, new, and unprecedented formulations of God's revelation to Israel, within and through the Torah.

Should Christians now receive these powerful propositions as mere statements of fact, when they were meant to change the world – and after all, did change the world? And should Jews listen politely, and treat as trivial, statements that Jesus offered as his torah, statements that he clearly meant to form Torah-teaching, as much as others of his day taught Torah-teaching – but much more! The more you listen, as though you had never before heard them, the more you will realize that he made very special claims in his own behalf, claims not to be accepted too facilely or sidestepped too courteously, as have Christians and Jews, respectively, over the centuries. Here is a man, this young man and his students, whom some admired, some hated, but none ignored. I think we owe him a serious hearing, and that means a fresh and interested encounter, not merely genuflection and obedience, on the one side, or a casual nod, on the other.

So I state very simply: I can see myself meeting this man and, with courtesy, arguing with him. It is my form of respect, the only compliment I crave from others, the only serious tribute I pay to the people I take seriously – and therefore respect and even love.

I can see myself not only meeting and arguing with him, taking up specific things he says and challenging him on the basis of our shared Torah, the Scriptures that Christians would later on adopt as the "Old Testament," but I can imagine myself also saying, "Friend, you go your way, I'll go mine. I wish you well – without me. Yours is not the Torah of Moses, and all I have from God, and all I ever need from God, is that one Torah of Moses."

We would meet, we would argue, we would part friends – but we would part. He would have gone his way, to Jerusalem and the place he believed God had prepared for him; I would have gone my way, home to my wife and children, my dog and my garden. He would have gone his way to glory, I my way to my duties and my responsibilities.

Matthew makes it easy for us to hear as fresh and wonderful what aforetimes seemed obvious and merely self-evident. He sets the scene with some simple statements: "He went up on the mountain, and when he sat down his disciples came to him. And he opened his mouth and taught them, saying ..." In these words, Matthew conjures the picture of a master of the Torah who now teaches the Torah to his disciples. Jesus sits down, which, we know from later writings about rabbis, was the customary indication that serious teaching was going to commence. Indeed, taking one's seat marked the beginning of the lesson. The disciples surround him, round about, and fall silent. The scene is one of dignity and formality. Jesus does not conduct a conversation; nor does he give a lecture; he speaks truths. The disciples listen, because, in due course, they will enter into the argument and analysis of these truths, challenging, clarifying, convincing themselves through sustained exchange. In this context, we have to understand the sense of the word "Torah."

It bears two meanings, one with a capital *T*, the other with a small *t*. Torah with a capital T stands for God's revelation to Moses at Mount Sinai. When we write "torah" with a small t, we mean, "the instruction of a master – in the context of the teaching of the Torah." It is a somewhat odd shift; what Jesus does is teach the Torah, and what he teaches also is torah. For his engagement with the Torah of Moses – and Matthew makes clear Jesus is profoundly engaged in Torah-learning – means that things that he will say also form a continuation, expansion, elaboration, and clarification, for instance, of the Torah. He is a teacher of the Torah, so in the framework of the Torah, he teaches the Torah and he himself adds to the Torah: so his is a labor of torah too.

That simple statement, then, describing Jesus as a Torah-teacher teaching his torah to his disciples, makes possible an argument on a single subject: what God wants of me. What God instructed Moses at Mount Sinai and what Moses wrote down in the Torah is our shared set of facts. A single problem, an agreed-upon agenda, a shared set of facts – these are the requirements for a serious and sustained argument: a dialogue. So here I try to tell the story of the grounds for that dissent, so to frame an account of how I should have argued with Jesus and tried to persuade him and those with him that their view of the Torah – of what God wants from humanity – at important and substantive points was wrong. And therefore, because that specific teaching was so broadly out of phase with the Torah and covenant of Sinai, I could not then follow him and do not now either. That is not because I am stubborn or unbelieving. It is because I believe God has given a different Torah from the one that Jesus teaches; and that Torah, the one Moses got at Sinai, stands in judgment of the torah of Jesus, as it dictates true and false, right and wrong, for all other torahs that people want to teach in God's name.

What I want to discuss with Jesus is how his teachings fit together with the Torah. Have I then raised a criterion of truth that serves my argument but not Jesus'? Hardly, since Jesus is explicit in claiming that he comes to fulfill the Torah and not to destroy it. In Matthew's words:

Think not that I have come to abolish the Torah and the prophets; I have come not to abolish them but to fulfil them. For truly I say to you, till heaven and earth pass away, not an iota, not a dot, will pass from the Torah until all is accomplished. Whoever then relaxes one of the least of these commandments and teaches men so, shall be called least in the kingdom of heaven; but he who does them and teaches them shall be called great in the kingdom of heaven. For I tell you, unless your righteousness exceeds that of the scribes and Pharisees, you will never enter the kingdom of heaven. (Matt 5:17–20)

So the Torah is a legitimate criterion of truth, since both parties to the argument share the same conviction. And it's an urgent question, because, as we'll see, Matthew's Jesus instructs people to violate at least three of the Ten Commandments. And I am going to ask Jesus to his face: How can you tell people to violate some of the Ten Commandments and yet claim to teach torah, let alone the Torah of Moses given by God at Sinai?

As a practicing and believing Jew addressing the figure of a man who, variously represented, also comes forth as a practicing and believing Jew, I therefore can ask whether what Jesus says accords with what the Torah of Sinai says. According to Matthew, Jesus and I – among all of faithful, covenanted Israel – believe God gives the Torah. Jesus and I, along with all those who count themselves as the children of Abraham, Isaac, and Jacob, believe it is our duty to fulfill the Torah. That explains why I think there can be a fair argument: one worked out on a level playing field. But argument and contention express serious respect, and I mean in every line of this book to pay my respect to a figure of considerable consequence.

I realize it is difficult for Christians today, as it was long ago, to make sense of the continued vitality of the Torah, that is, of Judaism. To explain Israel's "unbelief," Christians have called Jews "perfidious," meaning "unbelieving"; have regarded them as stubborn or stiff-necked; have imputed to them invincible ignorance. The Gospels divide Israel behind believers and connivers, and for twenty centuries, Jews, faithful to the Torah of Moses, were called Christ-killers. So there has been a certain impatience with us, eternal Israel, perhaps understandably so.

Turning the clock back to a particular point in the life of Jesus – when he was a teacher in Galilee, before the horror of his crucifixion, but also (from a Christian perspective) the redeeming miracle of his resurrection, – another position becomes possible, besides the ones of belief in or denial of Jesus as Christ. It is the position that I think most of Israel, familiar with Jesus when he lived and taught, did take, and the one I take in this book: neither to follow nor to conspire against, but only to say a polite no, and to go on to other matters. That position is plausible if we imagine ourselves in Galilee, hearing a master teach his torah, long before he has gone his way into history and eternity.

Well, then, is this meeting with Jesus in Galilee not an act of enormous disrespect? How dare I argue with the master at all? The answer is both personal and religious. I have lived a life of learning, and to me, if I didn't take the other's ideas seriously, I would agree facilely and go on my way, or I would condescend, or I would pretend and humor the other. The only teachers who ever taught me anything listened to my ideas and gave me their criticism, and they are the only ones I ever respected. The students I respect are the ones I mean to challenge through my careful attention to what they say, therefore my most rigorous response to their ideas: criticism.

But argument serves as more than a personal and perhaps idiosyncratic way of paying tribute; it certainly does not win much popularity, and one of my closest friends in politics calls me "the most contentious person I've ever known," which I took as a compliment and he meant as a compliment, for me in particular. A good solid argument also is represented by the Torah as the right way to address God, that is, as an act of enormous devotion. The founder of eternal Israel, Abraham, argued with God to save Sodom. Moses time and again argued with God. Many of the prophets took up the argument as well, Jeremiah for example. So ours – the Torah's – is a God that expects to be argued with; and the most profound affirmation of God's rule and will that the Torah contains – the book of Job – forms also a sustained and systematic argument with God.

So as a believer in the Torah, that is, in Judaism, I come in a different spirit altogether. In my religion, argument forms a mode of divine service, as much as prayer: reasoned debate on substantive issues, debate founded on respect for the other and made possible by shared premises. That kind of contention is not only a gesture of honor and respect for the other, but in the context of the Torah, it forms the gift of intellect on the altar of the Torah. I do not think a non-Christian can pay to him whom Christians know as Christ a more sincere tribute than a good, solid argument.

So much for the how of argument. But why compose such an argument? What makes it urgent at just this time, at the turn of the second millennium? For two thousand years people on either side more or less ignored the other. Judaism took for granted that Christianity never made a difference to the Torah. Christianity represented Judaism in so repulsive a form that, in all honesty, why should any honorable person have wanted to conduct a dialogue with that religion? So – why bother, just now, to take up an argument postponed for nearly two thousand years?

Bother, partly because religious dialogue in twenty-first-century America is going to take place; our native American curiosity and basic goodwill make it possible.

Bother, partly because in the free climate of American religion, Jews are asked to explain themselves, and in a mostly Christian country, this means, why are you not like us Christians?

Bother, partly because within the diverse Christianities of this country flourishes one that represents itself as a Judaism, "Messianic Judaism," observing Judaism (whole or in part) and believing also in Jesus as Christ.

So people want to know why they can't be both Jews and Christians simultaneously – and Judaism maintains that they cannot. Why not? What's wrong with Jesus? That formulation of matters, though unfortunate, proves natural in the world of profound intimacy – in mind and heart, intellect and sentiment – between Jews and Christians in which, because of America's free and open society, we now all flourish together.

At the same time, Christians find themselves drawn to Judaism in its own terms. And part of their interest in choosing Judaism is because Christianity leads them to Sinai (the "Old Testament"), which, for some, turns out to be the sole destination. So on both sides we witness these days not only the encounter of neighbors, but the claim of a meeting within the very house of Israel itself.

But there is yet another reason for the intimacy of dialogue contained in serious argument. Contention – as I said in defending the idea of having an argument with another religion – marks companions, and Jews and Christians now meet in marriage and the raising of their children. The house of Israel now shelters Christians, the offspring of Christians, and converts from Christianity to Judaism. Jews become Christians as much as Christians become Jews. And the Judaeo-Christian interchange takes place, these days, at home and in bed. For the marriage of Jews and Christians proceeds apace, with the result that intimacy in other ways now leads also to a sharing of religious convictions. Then where, in Christianity, are Jews to find a point of shared comprehension? And what have they to say for themselves when confronted by the confident claims of the dominant religion of this country?

From the perspective of our own religion, we Jews find exceedingly implausible fundamental convictions of the other. With many of these allegations it is difficult to contend, let alone conduct a reasoned argument. What are we to make, for example, of the notion that God has a mother, to whom God listens? How are we to understand the claim that, uniquely in all humankind, Jesus was God incarnate, "in our image, after our likeness," in the language of Genesis' account of the creation of man and woman, in a way in which no other human being has been in God's image: God incarnate? These and other fundamental beliefs of Christianity lie beyond all comprehending among those who stand outside of the faith.

For their part, rightly wanting to be understood, Christians find incomprehensible eternal Israel's sense of itself as well. For if Jews find the conception of God uniquely incarnate in one man to be beyond comprehending, Christians find the notion of God's people, Israel's election, behind all access. For neither side can imagine an analogy, within terms it can comprehend, to what is most sacred to the other. And these fundamentals, each essential to the self-understanding of believers, speak of what is unique – therefore, by definition, what can be grasped only intuitively. God incarnate, the election of Israel – these commanding truths of Christ, on the one side, Torah, on the other – cannot be subjected to reasoned argument between us and the other, for example, argument to settle questions about right and wrong, truth and falsity, a debate resting on shared premises and mutually agreed upon facts.

But that simple statement points to an impasse, one we cannot permanently accept. For shall we have nothing to say to our friends, our neighbors, and in not a few cases, our sons' and daughters' wives and husbands – or even our own children? And are they going to have nothing to say to us? Our situation in a free and open society, with people moving every which way, cannot sustain brute silence: you believe, we don't; or that's what you believe, this is what we believe.

There is yet another consideration for taking seriously the Christian argument with Judaism. Hearing twenty centuries of nay-saying, Christians naturally saw Jesus' own people, Israel, as stubborn and merely negative. But if the negative contains a powerful affirmation, as it does, still, there is more to Judaism in its meeting with Christianity than a mere no. There is a no, because ... And in that "because" dwells a mighty debate between us both. So in these pages I propose to show how Israel, the people of God, would appear if a reasoned argument between things Jesus taught and teachings of the Torah could be conceived. What I mean is an argument on the substance of things, as though all that mattered were what is true by the criterion accepted by both parties: the Torah.

But what are the rules for a shared and fair debate? First of all, both parties must speak to the same issue. Therefore, as I have now explained in terms of home and family, I choose an account of Jesus shaped for Israel in particular to confront – the Gospel of Matthew. Since Matthew's particular portrait of Jesus came from a Jewish group, was addressed to the rest of Israel, and emphasized how he had come not to destroy but to fulfill the Torah, a genuine debate can take place. The reason is that here, and here alone, a genuinely shared premise – the Torah – stands in judgment upon all teachings and actions, establishing the basis for argument: the possibility of appeal to a single source of truth. About what can eternal Israel argue with Paul or John? For them, questions are settled, which Matthew's Jesus opens up. Paul's Jesus has risen from the dead; John's Jesus stands outside of Israel altogether, with "the Jews" portrayed as the other and the enemy. But Matthew's Jesus is portrayed as one of us.

Second, each party to the debate has to concede the other's integrity. Nearly the whole of the Christian polemical literature on Judaism, and most of Christian scholarship on Judaism even in our own times, denies to Judaism all trace of honor. With that literature, religious dialogue is unthinkable. Not only should we not have reason to talk with them, but, monsters as they portray Judaism, why should they want to talk with us? For example, I cannot conceive an argument with John's Jesus, because eternal Israel in John is treated with unconcealed hatred. But here in Matthew's Gospel that is not the case.

Matthew presents more than a supernatural figure. His Jesus of the House of David not only performed miracles but died, spent three days in Hell, then rose from the dead and left an empty tomb. Matthew's writing also offers, as evidence for why I should accept Jesus as Christ, the teachings that Jesus put forth while here on earth, among us. It is right and proper, therefore, for me to examine some of those teachings and to ask whether they compel me, within eternal Israel, to accept them as part of the Torah. And that is precisely what I propose to do. In doing so, I concede as valid the deeply held convictions of the other that lie beyond the bounds of an outsider's examination; or I set them aside as not germane to the case to which I am asked to respond: take your choice.

Third, each party to the debate owes the other respect. Christians who worship Jesus Christ will probably view as an odd form of respect this sustained argument with the man they revere as God incarnate, and they are not wrong. In the literature of Judaic polemics against Christianity and Christian polemics against Judaism, no one before now has insisted we argue about the same things, and only those things, appealing to the same criterion of truth, and only that. That makes this book odd. But still, how can I argue with God incarnate? Well, as I said, once God incarnate says to do one thing rather than some other, appealing to the Torah as validation for that statement, then it is right and proper to take issue.

Once again, in Judaism, argument forms a principal means of religious discourse: it is how we talk with one another, the way in which we show our esteem and respect for the other. A principal religious activity in Judaism requires "study of the Torah," and much of Torah-study requires contention: dispute and argument on propositions, evidence, validity of analysis, what we do in every realm of learning. I spend my life in study of the Torah (in a particular way) and am used to this union of my religious commitment, expressed in a serious confrontation with the intellect and ideas of the other, and my secular vocation, which requires me seriously to confront the viewpoint of the other.

In this respect I do ask Christians to adopt one trait of the Judaic tradition. Like Christians, we value reason and reasoned faith, forming one of the great intellectual traditions of humanity in our holy books. The single most influential book of Judaism is the Talmud of Babylonia (ca. A.D. 600), which is a sustained commentary on a philosophical law code called the Mishnah (ca. A.D. 200). That Talmud is simply one long argument, or rather, it is notes on how today we can reconstruct the argument they had

29

long ago. And from the time that that Talmud reached final form, everyone who studied the writing not only listened to the argument but tried to participate. The religious life of the Torah – that is, of Judaism – therefore takes the form of a long, long argument about this and that. Other people spend long hours reciting Psalms or saying prayers, and many Jews do that too. But the really elite of our faith, the masters (and now, mistresses too!) of the Torah, spend long hours arguing about statements of the Torah, as these are put forth in the Mishnah and the Talmud. That is our highest action in the service of God, once we have done our duty to our fellow human beings.

Why so? Because we regard the use of the mind, the interchange of thought, proposition, reason, evidence, analysis – we regard argument as an exercise in the use of what we share with God, what makes us like God, which is our minds. I would gladly argue with God, just as the great rabbis of the Talmud did, if occasion arose; so why not with someone else's God incarnate? How better pay respect to that religion and that figure than offer my best in response to his best?

So as I said, argument is a gesture of respect, not offense. Abraham met God head-on at Sodom; Moses insisted on seeing God, even in the cleft of the rock; the prophets and Job, after all, form part of our Torah (too). And the oral Torah that we have from Sinai – that teaches us the rules of reasoned argument about holy things, among people who believe that we serve God by our exercise of applied reason and practical logic in the study of the Torah. When we go to Heaven, some of us at least hope to join the academy up there, the Heavenly Yeshiva, and to join in the arguments of Moses, our rabbi, and the great sages.

In the context of that religion, there is no greater gesture of respect than an argument. I reject that mode of Judaeo-Christian dialogue that, for centuries, on the Judaic side, consisted in (1) claiming Christianity really doesn't exist; (2) alleging that, if Christianity exists, it never made a difference to Judaism (in the language of Judaism: to "the Torah"); and (3) telling nasty stories about the person Jesus. I look with disgust at writings that defame religions and holy women and men of religions, sharing the outrage of Islam with the Muslim perception of Rushdie's *Satanic Verses* (whether that perception conforms to reality or not being no issue here), sharing the sense of deep offense that Christians take at the vile representations of Jesus that these days win considerable attention. In service on public, decision-making bodies, I identified with the position of Christians who took issue with the use of public funds for the defamation of their faith and its founder. The public record is clear: I paid the price, and gladly at that.

So my intent is not to give offense, only to take issue. That again explains why I isolate for debate only the this-worldly component of a wholly supernatural figure – and no one can encounter Matthew's Jesus without concurring that before us in the evangelist's mind is God incarnate. In every line of these pages I realize I am writing about somebody else's God, to whom prayer and devotion and lives of service are sanctified, not a man but God incarnate, to whom vast masses of humanity turn with their hope for life eternal.

In no way do I call into question the faith of the faithful. Nor is it the place of the outsider to stand in judgment upon the faith of other people. I should be proud if Christian readers responded, "Yes, we have considered the issues you raise, and having thought about them and argued with you in our minds, we affirm with greater faith than ever our belief in Jesus Christ." And nothing would make me happier than to hear from Jewish readers, "Now I understand why we are what we are; and I am proud to be what we are."

This is not an argument I want to win. It is an argument to make plausible to both Jews and Christians that other position, the one of the Torah, that Jews have affirmed in the nearly two thousand years since they went their own way and chose not to follow Jesus at all. This I say without apology, without deceit or guile. What I do is simply reaffirm the Torah of Sinai over against Matthew's Jesus Christ: Moses would want no less of any of us, or Matthew's Jesus, I think, no more. So when I say, if I heard those words that day, I would have offered an argument, it is with the living, mortal man, walking among us and talking with us, that I set forth my argument. If all I had in hand were these words, out of the context of genealogy, miracle, crucifixion, resurrection, and enthronement at the right hand of God, what should I have found as response? Not yes but ... , nor praise for the great teacher and rabbi, nor even affirmation that, if not the Messiah, well, then, a prophet – none of these. It is disingenuous to offer Jesus a standing, within Judaism, that Christianity rightly finds trivial and beside the point. If not Messiah, God incarnate, then to what grand issue of faith does my affirmation of a rabbi's or a prophet's teaching pertain?

These concessions express a disingenuous evasion of the issue. They mask a most sincere denial: Jesus can be conceded to have been anything but what Christianity has claimed, which is – at the very least – Christ, Messiah, God incarnate. So neither in times past nor in our own day has much of a solid argument been attempted with that component of Christianity's Jesus Christ, God incarnate, that Judaism may confront: you think, I think, here's why. Several generations of Jewish apologists have fulsomely praised this "Galilean miracle worker," placing him in the tradition of Elijah and the Hasidic rabbis of the eighteenth century and afterward. Other generations have praised Jesus as a great rabbi. These evasions of the Christian claim to truth will serve no more. Christianity does not believe in a Galilean miracle worker, nor does Christianity worship a rabbi. For my part, I will not evade. I will not concede. I will not praise with excessive, irrelevant compliments someone else's God: it is demeaning and dishonest.

So to conclude, by addressing teachings of Jesus as Matthew portrays him, I pay the tribute of serious attention to what, until now, has found little serious attention among Jews. For until our own century, Jews have dismissed Christianity without paying much attention to what Jesus in particular taught. From the first century to our own time, when Jews have responded to Jesus, it was to Christianity as a whole, its rich and complex picture of the man and his meaning, that they replied. In full knowledge of what would happen afterward – from the Christian perspective, his death and resurrection, the founding of his Church, the expansion of that Church across the face of the entire world – Jews could scarcely imagine, and rarely undertook, the more modest, but more plausible, exchange of ideas set forth as one component of the case for Jesus as Christ. Let me try.

Rather than criticizing Matthew's story of Jesus in the manner of scholars, let us appreciate it, imagine ourselves participants in it. For Matthew was a great storyteller, which is proved by the simple fact that, from his time to ours, readers have responded with deep emotion to the story that he tells. So why can't we appreciate, enter into the story too? From here on, I dispense with the proper acknowledgement of scholarship, "Matthew's Jesus." This is not a book of scholarship – I don't even list the books I read in trying to understand Matthew's Gospel, and this isn't really a book about Matthew's Gospel at all. This is a book about faith meeting faith, and anyhow, everyone understands that Matthew's Jesus is only one account of – one road toward – the Jesus who actually lived and taught, did wonders and miracles, raised up disciples, was persecuted under Pontius Pilate, crucified, raised from the dead, and now is enthroned on high. So Matthew's road is just one.

But I want to read it, as part of the Christians' Bible, the way the faithful do in the Churches and, by the way, the way Jews do when they open the New Testament – in that manner, and not in the quite valid reading of theologians in the academy and in seminaries. My argument is with the Jesus that faithful Christians revere, the one known to them in the great narratives, among them, that one written to Jews in particular. Now, then, we join in the story Matthew tells about Jesus, speaking now of the things the storyteller tells us as though they were out there, before us. We know only two things: the Torah and Matthew's story of things Jesus said – nothing more.

"Seeing the crowds, he went up on the mountain, and when he sat down his disciples came to him. And he opened his mouth and taught them, saying ... " We come without further ado to that mountain in Galilee where Jesus presented the heart of his teachings. We stand at the foot of the mountain. Looking upward, we see the figure of the man. He says many things. We can grasp just some of them – we, eternal Israel, remembering that other mountain – Sinai – and what God told Moses to tell us there.

3

Not to Destroy but to Fulfill

vs

You Have Heard That It Was Said, but I Say to You

"Think not that I have come to abolish the Torah and the prophets; I have come not to abolish them but to fulfill them. For truly I say to you, till heaven and earth pass away, not an iota, not a dot, will pass from the Torah until all is accomplished. Whoever then relaxes one of the least of these commandments and teaches men so, shall be called least in the kingdom of heaven; but he who does them and teaches them shall be called great in the kingdom of heaven. For I tell you, unless your righteousness exceeds that of the scribes and Pharisees, you will never enter the kingdom of heaven."

Matthew 5:17–20

It would not take a long journey to meet the master. He was everywhere. But to hear the message whole, I had to wait until the day he ascended a mountain and talked there to his disciples, in the hearing of outsiders as well. For my part, drawn by curiosity about how the Torah would govern life in my time and place, I came too.

And it was well that I did. For the sayings he said that day, now reaching us as the Sermon on the Mount, reported in Matthew 5:1–7:29, form Jesus' principal statement of teachings. These comprise well-ordered propositions with which one may argue – as distinct from Jesus' miracles, the story of his life, the things he did, and of course, his suffering on the Cross, death, and resurrection: "He is not here, for he has risen" (Matt 28:6). All these parts of the Gospel, that is, "good news," make sense to believers, since it is to the faithful that Matthew tells the good news. But seated with his disciples on the mountain, Jesus teaches them – and us bystanders as well – his torah. Here is where and how he tells people how things are, what they should do, how God wants us to live. And Jesus' torah is substantial and, by his own word, controversial too. So he invites argument and opens the way to contention, as every teacher does who wants to change people's minds – not to say, their lives too. So let me join the argument on those specific matters that address my life and world, framed at Sinai.

When we first hear from Jesus, rather than merely about him, he is telling people about God's kingdom. This for me is a homely concern, one that the Torah has made mine too. When I accept the yoke of the commandments of the Torah and do them, I accept God's rule. I live in the kingdom of God, which is to say, in the dominion of Heaven, here on earth. That is what it means to live a holy life: to live by the will of God in the here and now.

From the perspective of eternal Israel and its covenant with God, this message surely wins our goodwill, since the Torah lays out the life of Israel as a kingdom of priests and holy people, under the rule of God through the prophet, Moses himself, and through the divinely ordained priesthood, founded by Aaron, Moses' brother. When we recite "Hear O Israel, the Lord our God, the Lord is one," which is called the "Shema (Deut 6:4–9)," from the opening word, "Hear," we tell ourselves that we thereby "accept the yoke of the kingdom of heaven," as the teachers of the Torah say. That is to say, we accept the commandments that

God has given to us in the covenant of Sinai. Not only so, but when Jesus proposes to teach Torah to Israel, important parts of his torah fall well within the range of familiar topics. At the outset, moreover, he announces his purpose is not to abolish the Torah and the prophets but to fulfill them. The Torah remains valid: that is his message, and on that basis, I come to listen. He has every right to a careful hearing.

I stand there, hear words that move me, listen confidently. For Jesus' first words win my confidence. Jesus opens his preaching of the gospel of the kingdom with a message with which no disciple of Moses' Torah would take exception: "blessed are the poor in spirit, for theirs is the kingdom of heaven; blessed are the meek, for they shall inherit the earth" (Matt 5:3). "Blessed are those who hunger and thirst for righteousness, for they shall be satisfied. Blessed are the merciful, for they shall obtain mercy. Blessed are the pure in heart, for they shall see God. Blessed are the peacemakers, for they shall be called sons of God" (Matt 5:6–9). I cannot imagine taking issue with teachings such as these, which keep the promise of the Torah: "he who does them and teaches them shall be called great in the kingdom of heaven."

But in the context defined by Matthew, what comes next? "Blessed are you when men revile you and persecute you and utter all kinds of evil against you falsely on my account. Rejoice and be glad, for your reward is great in heaven, for so men persecuted the prophets who were before you" (Matt 5:11–12). Why should anyone persecute the disciples of someone who blesses the pure in heart and peacemakers and the poor in spirit? But Jesus' attention has now shifted from the poor in spirit, the mourners, the meek, those who hunger and thirst for righteousness and who are merciful, to "you." This is jarring, and it catches my interest. Listening carefully, I hear echoes of controversy, but see no cause for it. For the "you" has shifted from all of us Jews, today's eternal Israel, standing there, to those who are persecuted "on my account." Nothing in the master's message leads me to take exception to anything he has said; to the contrary, the Torah makes ample provision for the poor, those who mourn, the meek, those who hunger and thirst for righteousness. The Torah teaches us to show mercy. So none of these teachings explain why this particular master should warn me that I will be persecuted on account of following him.

By way of assurance, I hear, "Think not that I have come to abolish the Torah and the prophets; I have come not to abolish them but to fulfill them." And what this must mean is that if there is rejection or persecution, it is not because anything I hear from him conflicts with what I hear from Sinai. So whence the persecution, why the consolation for suffering on his account? In fact, the sage on the mountain himself identifies the reason. The contrast between the message echoing from Sinai and the one announced today is drawn explicitly. So I am told to expect to hear something fresh, original, and superior to anything that has gone before – and yet, torah in conformity with the Torah revealed by God to Moses at Sinai. So the sage sets for himself a worthy challenge, one that every sage in every generation does well to meet: receive a tradition whole and perfect, hand it on never intact but always unimpaired, so taking a rightful place in the chain of tradition from Sinai.

For it is the task of each generation both to receive and to hand on, in the language of the opening sentence of Mishnah-tractate Abot, sayings of the Founders of Judaism. The Mishnah is a philosophical law code, completed around A.D. 200, which is the first authoritative and canonical writing in Judaism after the Hebrew Scriptures. The Judaism that appeals to the Mishnah recognizes no holy book written between the Hebrew Scriptures or "Old Testament" and that document, and all later holy books begin with either Scripture or the Mishnah. So that is the most important writing in Judaism after the Torah. The tractate in hand sets forth principles of the faith and important rules of conduct. The composition begins with this language:

Moses received Torah at Sinai and handed it on to Joshua, Joshua to elders, and elders to prophets. And prophets handed it on to the men of the great assembly. They said three things: "Be prudent in judgment. Raise up many disciples. Make a fence for the Torah."

It is right and proper, therefore, for this sage both to receive but also to hand on meaning, to take over the heritage of Sinai, and also to hand over to the next generation something that this sage has added to the heritage of Sinai. Since, we note, what the men of the great assembly say is not to cite Scripture but to contribute their own teaching to the chain of tradition, it is easy for me to expect from Jesus not merely a reprise or paraphrase of Scripture, but something fresh and new, and yet wholly part of that received Torah – now handed on. I am prepared for what he offers: to receive the Torah, but also to hear this master's renewal of the Torah.

I therefore find myself at home as a sequence of lessons is set forth, each of them prefaced by the statement that other, prior masters teach a lesser truth, but Jesus, a greater one. These are what is meant by not abolishing but fulfilling the Torah and the prophets, and among them five important ones capture my attention:

1 "You have heard that it was said …'You shall not kill …' But I say to you that every one who is angry with his brother shall be liable …" (Matt 5:21–22)

2 "You have heard that it was said, 'You shall not commit adultery.' But I say to you that every one who looks at a woman lustfully has already committed adultery with her in his heart." (Matt 5:27–28)

3 "Again you have heard that it was said to the men of old, 'You shall not swear falsely, but shall perform to the Lord what you have sworn.' But I say to you, Do not swear at all" (Matt 5:33–34)

4 "You have heard that it was said, 'An eye for an eye and a tooth for a tooth.' But I say to you, Do not resist one who is evil. But if any one strikes you on the right cheek, turn to him the other also …" (Matt 5:38–39)

39

5 "You have heard that it was said, 'You shall love your neighbor and hate your enemy.' But I say to you, Love your enemies and pray for those who persecute you ... You, therefore, must be perfect, as your heavenly Father is perfect." (Matt 5:43–4, 48)

We have to distinguish the substance of what Jesus is saying from the form that he gives to his statements. The message justifies my confidence but, of course, leaves me more puzzled than ever about what can be controversial in what are wise and deep readings of Torah-statements: a torah – the teaching of a master – that finds a comfortable place in the Torah – the revelation of God to Moses at Mount Sinai, a revelation that makes a place for the teaching of acknowledged sages through all of time. For what Jesus accomplishes in these sayings is to point at the center and heart of the Torah's message.

Specifically, Jesus sets forth as his demonstration of how not to abolish the Torah and the prophets but to fulfill them a set of teachings that, all together, point to a more profound demand – on the Torah's part – than people have realized. Not only must I not kill, I must not even approach that threshold of anger that in the end leads to murder. Not only must I not commit adultery, I must not even approach the road that leads to adultery. Not only must I not swear falsely by God's name, I should not swear at all. These formulations represent an elaboration of three of the Ten Commandments (later on we shall meet two more of them). In the language of a text of Judaism attributed to authorities long before Jesus' own time, "Make a fence around the Torah." That is to say, conduct yourself in such a way that you will avoid even the things that cause you to sin, not only sin itself.

By seeking reconciliation, I make a fence against wanting to kill; by chastity in thought, against adultery in deed; by not swearing, against not swearing falsely. Here is a message well worth hearing, one that makes plausible the somewhat odd contrast between what I have heard and what I now hear. But that is a good device to win my attention, and it has, and I am impressed – and moved. To be sure, rabbis in the great rabbinic documents would in time come to the same conclusion, to avoid anger, to avoid temptation, to avoid vowing and swearing, but that fact is not germane to our argument. What is relevant is that many of the teachings of the wisdom writings and prophecy, Proverbs for example, will lead to these same laudable conclusions; for example, the Lord hates a false witness, not to desire the beauty of an evil woman in your heart and not to let her capture you with her eyelashes (Prov 6:25–26), and the like.

Not only so, but the teaching of the Torah by a paraphrase of the Torah would form a staple of rabbis' teaching later on. For we have access to a great master, Yohanan ben Zakkai (the name is strange; in English, Yohanan is John, and "ben Zakkai" can be rendered "the righteous"; hence "John the righteous," which makes him somewhat less exotic). In sayings associated with him and his disciples, we have exactly the same program: restate in concrete terms, and in a more profound setting, the requirements of the Torah of Sinai. A brief glimpse at how he taught his disciples, and how they too paraphrased the teachings of the Torah in such a way as to make them more concrete and more profound at the same time, will show why I find myself so comfortable as I hear the words from the mount in Galilee:

> Rabban Yohanan b. Zakkai received [the Torah] from Hillel and Shammai. He would say, "If you have learned much Torah, do not puff yourself up on that account, for it was for that purpose that you were created."
>
> He had five disciples, and these are they: Rabbi Eliezer b. Hyrcanus, Rabbi Joshua b. Hananiah, Rabbi Yosé the priest, Rabbi Simeon b. Netanel, and Rabbi Eleazar b. Arakh.
>
> He said to them, "Go and see what is the straight path to which someone should stick."
>
> Rabbi Eliezer says, "Good will."

Rabbi Joshua says, "A good friend."

Rabbi Yosé says, "A good neighbor."

Rabbi Simeon says, "Foresight."

Rabbi Eleazar says, "A generous spirit."

He said to them, "I prefer the opinion of Rabbi Eleazar b. Arakh, because in what he says is included everything you say."

He said to them, "Go out and see what is the bad road, which someone should avoid."

Rabbi Eliezer says, "Envy."

Rabbi Joshua says, "A bad friend."

Rabbi Yosé says, "A bad neighbor."

Rabbi Simeon says, "Defaulting on a loan."

Rabbi Eleazar says, "An ungenerous spirit."

He said to them, "I prefer the opinion of Rabbi Eleazar b. Arakh, because in what he says is included everything you say."

They [each] said three things.

Rabbi Eliezer says, "Let the respect owing to your fellow be as precious to you as the respect owing to you yourself. And don't be easy to anger. And repent one day before you die."

Rabbi Yosé says, "Let your fellow's property be as precious to you as your own. And get yourself ready to learn Torah, for it does not come as an inheritance to you. And may everything you do be for the sake of Heaven." (Mishnah-tractate Abot 2:8ff.)

If I wanted to explain the meaning of the great commandment of Leviticus 19: 18, "You will love your neighbor as yourself," I could not do better than turn to the disciples of Yohanan ben Zakkai. The final sayings draw me closest to that amplification: "loving my neighbor as myself" means that I have to take care of my neighbor's honor as much as the honor owing to me, my neighbor's property as much as my own. Neither Jesus nor the disciples of Yohanan ben Zakkai cite verses of Scripture or prooftexts. The disciples simply state their own propositions in response to the master's question; the operative verse of Scripture, Leviticus 19:18, is not quoted, but it is very present. Represented as Matthew presents Jesus, we should have something like this:

"You have heard it said, 'You will love your neighbor as yourself,' but I say to you, Let the respect owing to your fellow be as precious to you as the respect owing to you yourself.'

"You have heard it said, 'You will love your neighbor as yourself,' but I say to you, Let your fellow's property be as precious to you as your own."

Now when I say that the message wins my confidence, but the form is jarring, you understand what I mean. In calling upon the Torah and explaining how a true understanding of its intent requires more than people now understand, Jesus' torah meets that challenge that sages set for themselves, which is not only to receive the Torah, but also to hand it on. And that means not only to repeat or to paraphrase, but to teach, explain, extend, amplify, enrich. And in these sayings, that is precisely what Jesus accomplishes.

That is not to say that everything I hear in the language "You have heard, but I say ..." gains such immediate assent: familiar, but better. I look in vain in some of his statements for such obvious confirmation of Jesus' claim that he has come not to destroy but to fulfill. For the fourth and the fifth statements present a different problem. Not to resist evil? The message of the Torah and the prophets holds the opposite. No one, of course, imagined that exact, physical retribution would be exacted; monetary compensation for personal injury surprises no one.

But not resisting one who is evil has no relationship to "an eye for an eye." This is not in the category of "a fence around the Torah." It is a religious duty to resist evil, to struggle for good, to love God, and to fight against those who make themselves into enemies of God. The Torah knows nothing of not resisting evil and does not value either the craven person, who submits, or the arrogant person, who holds that it is beneath one's dignity to deign to oppose evil. Passivity in the face of evil serves the cause of evil. The Torah calls eternal Israel always to struggle for God's purpose; the Torah sanctions warfare and recognizes legitimate power. So I find amazing Jesus' statement that it is a religious duty to fold before evil.

True, Proverbs teaches, "A soft answer turns away wrath" (Prov 15:1). Anyone who knew that verse will have identified with Jesus' expansion of it. Nor should we ignore, "If your enemy is hungry, give him bread to eat; and if he is thirsty, give him water to drink; for you will heap coals of fire on his head, and the Lord will reward you" (Prov 25:21–22). But that rather shrewd counsel hardly prepares us for, "Do not resist one who is evil," which demands something else altogether.

The fifth statement cites a saying not to be found in the Torah, which contains no commandment to hate one's enemies. The torah of later rabbis held: hate the evil, not the evildoer. Anyone who knows the Torah will wonder where we are supposed to have heard that "commandment," which God did not command Moses to tell us. But God's enemies are another matter, and these we do resist – and in other parts of the narrative, so does Jesus. Not only so, but the Torah clearly tells us to fight against the enemies of God: Amalek, for example, Korach for instance, among many.

How to make sense of these two items? I find much wisdom in the observation of C. G. Montefiore: "Jesus was not thinking of public justice, the order of civic communities, the organization of states, but only how the members of his religious brotherhood should act towards each other and towards those outside their ranks. Public justice is outside of his purview."* If, then, Jesus meant to instruct his circle of disciples, seated around him, to turn the other cheek, to let the other have one's cloak, to go the extra mile – well, who can differ? That is the road of forebear-

* *The Synoptic Gospels* (New York: Ktav Publishing House, 1968 [repr. of 1927 ed.]), p.71.

ance, which, after all, Yohanan's disciples brought back as the good way too: a liberal, forgiving spirit above all. But then, the message is not to the people at the foot of the hill, but only to those seated at the top. In that context, we find ourselves back where we were when we noticed how much Jesus focused his teaching on "us," the little group of disciples who took their seats about him at the top of the mountain, while the rest of us stood down below.

Jesus addresses not eternal Israel, but a group of disciples. His focus, time and again, defines a limited vision. But eternal Israel comes forth from Sinai not a collection of families, but something more: a collectivity that adds up to much more than the sum of the parts, much more than families, but rather, a people, a nation, a society: "a kingdom of priests and a holy people." As the teaching unfolds, I begin to wonder whether there is not a missed mark here – not a sin, but not a target squarely hit either. Jesus on the mountain addresses not "all Israel," this one and that one, individuals and families. He speaks to our lives, but not to the whole of the world in which we make those lives. For we find ourselves hearing a message for home and hearth, for growing up and growing old – but not for community, state, an ongoing social order, such as eternal Israel comprises in this world.

As we shall observe later on, so we notice right at the outset, Jesus sees the poor, the mourners, the meek, the merciful, the peacemakers. And all those form part of eternal Israel, perhaps from God's perspective, the best part. But I listen for a message to not me alone, or my life and my family, but to all of us, eternal Israel, who stood at Sinai not as a motley mob but as God's people, children of Abraham, Isaac, and Jacob. Jesus himself – so Matthew tells me – is son of David son of Abraham. But when he stands on the mountain, that is not the audience he sees.

But it is the audience in which I take my part. That is what I mean by a missed mark. So much for the substance: much with merit, but the silences prove ominous. We – eternal Israel – need

45

torah to tell us what God wants of us. But Jesus has spoken only about how I, in particular, can do what God wants of me. In the shift from the "us" of Sinai to the "I" of the torah of the Galilean sage Jesus takes an important step – in the wrong direction. And if I had been there, I would have wondered what he had to say to not me but to us: all Israel, assembled, that day, in the persons present, before him to hear his torah.

But if the substance strikes me as both meritorious and flawed, the form is precisely what Matthew says: amazing. If I were there, would I have shared in the astonishment of the crowds? Yes, and for the very reason Matthew gives, "For he taught them as one who had authority, and not as their scribes."

The wording "You have heard it said" leaves open the question: "By whom? For what?" A teacher of the Torah is judged by the Torah and responsible to it. Then, surely, when the Torah is at issue, a clear reference to the Torah is called for. And the circumlocution here proves disingenuous. For who does not know that "it was said to the men of old" refers to what God said to Moses at Sinai? Jesus knows that up there on the mountain, and I know it, and everyone around me knows it. For that thing I have heard in fact is what God says to Moses in the Torah: "You shall not murder, you shall not commit adultery, you shall not take the name of the Lord your God in vain," and other of the Ten Commandments. So here again, the valid claim to interpret what the Torah says is joined with a puzzling formulation indeed.

Yes, I would have been astonished. Here is a Torah-teacher who says in his own name what the Torah says in God's name. It is one thing to say on one's own how a basic teaching of the Torah shapes the everyday: "Let the other's honor ... the property ... be as precious to you as your own ..." It is quite another to say that the Torah says one thing, but I say ... then to announce in one's own name what God set forth at Sinai. That explains both why I would have wondered and why I would have also taken pleasure in the teachings of a teacher of the Torah who also enriched my understanding of some of the things that God had given in the Torah, specifically in explaining how to make a fence about some of the Ten Commandments, how to conduct my life in such a way as to show my faith in God and in God's providence: "Do not boast about tomorrow, for you do not know what a day may bring forth" (Prov 27:1), and the like.

For what kind of torah is it that improves upon the teachings of the Torah without acknowledging the source – and it is God who is the Source – of those teachings? I am troubled not so much by the message, though I might take exception to this or that, as I am by the messenger. The reason is that, in form these statements are jarring. Standing on the mountain, Jesus' use of language, "You have heard that it was said ... but I say to you ..." contrasts strikingly with Moses' language at Mount Sinai. Sages, we saw, say things in their own names, but without claiming to improve upon the Torah. The prophet, Moses, speaks not in his own name but in God's name, saying what God has told him to say. Jesus speaks not as a sage nor as a prophet. Note, when Moses turns to the people at Mount Sinai, he starts with these words: "I am the Lord your God who brought you out of the Land of Egypt, out of the house of bondage." Moses speaks as God's prophet, in God's name, for God's purpose. So how am I to respond to this "I," who pointedly contrasts what I have heard said with what he says?

Now in his story, Matthew himself points to this contrast, "for he taught them as one who had authority, and not as their scribes." Moses alone had authority. The scribes teach the message and meaning of what Moses had set down as the Torah on the authority of God. So we find ourselves right where we started: with the difficulty of making sense, within the framework of the Torah, of a teacher who stands apart from, perhaps above, the Torah. At many points in this protracted account of Jesus' specific teachings, we now recognize that at issue is the figure of Jesus, not the teachings at all.

47

So, time and again, in the context of their relationship with him, the disciples are told: "Blessed are you when men revile you and persecute you and utter all kinds of evil against you falsely on my account" (Matt 5:11); "Not every one who says to me, 'Lord, Lord,' shall enter the kingdom of heaven, but he who does the will of my Father who is in heaven" (Matt 7:21); "Every one then who hears these words of mine and does them will be like a wise man who built his house upon a rock" (Matt 7:24) These statements and many like them address not eternal Israel but only those Israelites (and others) who acknowledge that "me," who refers to "my Father," and who can speak of "these words of mine." All these things are of a single cloth. At Sinai, God spoke through Moses. On this Galilean hill, Jesus speaks for himself. Moses spoke for God to "us," "eternal Israel," and we, Israel, responded as "we": "we shall do, we shall obey." In Galilee, Jesus speaks to crowds who are astonished at his teaching, identifying in the crowds the special hearers, those revealed on his account, individuals among eternal Israel, hearing this master addressing them, as he says, not as "their" (those others', those outsiders') scribes, "but as one who had authority."

In time to come, I would find the courage to approach the master and walk with him and talk with him. But here, in this first meeting, I keep my thoughts to myself. But what troubles me is simple, and if I could have walked up the mountain and addressed the master and disciples that day, I would have said: "Sir, how come you speak on your own say-so, and not out of the teachings of the Torah given by God to Moses at Sinai? It looks as though you see yourself as Moses, or as more than Moses. But the Torah of Moses does not tell me that God is going to give instruction – torah – through someone besides Moses or the other prophets; or that there is going to be another Torah. So I don't really know what to make of this claim of yours. You are an 'I,' but the Torah speaks only to a 'we,' to the 'us' of Israel, including you."

So even on that first day, it begins to dawn on me that if I don't already believe in this "I" who stands over against the Torah, I must find exceedingly difficult understanding the address I am hearing. And that accounts for that particular focus, the "you" who are going to be persecuted on "my" account, as though the mass of people standing at the foot of the mountain had faded into the Galilean hills. Where, in this Galilean scene, is the presence, here and now, of eternal Israel? In the scene before us, Jesus starts with a message to all Israel, but – as we've seen now – he shades over into an address to only that part of Israel that belongs to him. No wonder the narrator tells us, when Jesus finished his teachings, the crowds were amazed. But by the criterion of the Torah, Jesus has asked for what the Torah does not accord to anyone but God.

Not only so, but again and again Jesus places a wall between himself and other Israelites, whom he calls hypocrites. "Thus, when you give alms, sound no trumpet before you, as the hypocrites do in the synagogues and in the streets, that they may be praised by men" (Matt 6:2). "And when you pray, you must not be like the hypocrites; for they love to stand and pray in the synagogues and at the street corners, that they may be seen by men ... But when you pray, go into your room and shut the door and pray to your Father who is in secret; and your Father who sees in secret will reward you" (Matt 6:5–6).

Before proceeding, let me digress to respond to these criticisms of public piety. These sayings by themselves contain both valid criticism of an excess of public piety but also a rejection of the life of Israel, the community. It is one thing to condemn hypocrites, both for their ostentatious charity and their showy piety. Certainly Israel the eternal people, ancient and modern as well, has its share of hypocrites, people who celebrate themselves through their piety. But it is quite another thing to say that authentic prayer takes place only individually, only privately, only in secret. If what Jesus meant was that public prayer is improper, then he has called into question the Torah's fundamental premise, which is that Israel serves God not one by one but all together and all at once.

True, the Torah recognizes prayer offered by individuals, entirely on their own. But the Torah also calls upon Israel to serve God in community, in the Temple, for example, and the notion that the only valid prayer is offered up in secret is something that the Torah surely will find difficult to sustain. In a statement such as this, Jesus calls into question the entire tradition of prayer in community, of the "we" of Israelite prayer. It is one thing to reject what is done in public because people flaunt their piety. I have seen in synagogues, but also in churches, ample reason to wonder about such piety. It is quite another to dismiss as null the practice of public worship.

So, to revert to the point at which we started, how, in the framework of the Torah, do I respond to the specific statements of right and wrong, truth and falsehood, that Jesus has made this morning? I want to compose an argument on a level playing field, appealing to a common set of facts – the Torah's facts. But the Torah does not prepare me for a message contrasting what the Torah has said with what "I" say, nor does the Torah help me to understand a message framed in such a way that the very source of the teaching that has been said, the Torah itself, is sidestepped. The entire revelation at Sinai is now relegated to "it was said." And this in contrast to "I."

And, finally, the Torah came to all Israel, assembled at the foot of Sinai. But this torah seems special to those who believe, up front, in the one who teaches this torah – and who believe about that master not that he has mastered the Torah, but that he speaks, pretty much, on his own account, as someone who reveals what God wants. I walk away both much taken with fresh, profound insight into some of the Ten Commandments, and also deeply troubled. Clearly, something is at stake in this torah that is not at stake in the Torah-teaching of John the Righteous and his disciples.

Happily, being there on the spot, I have a chance to find my way toward the front of the crowd, and not at all shy, I plant myself just in the way in which the teacher is walking. "Sir, may I ask you a question?"

"Ask."

"Could we talk about what you said this morning, the main point, not the details?"

"So what do you think is my main point?"

"You say this: 'Think not that I have come to abolish the Torah and the prophets; I have come not to abolish them but to fulfill them.' But if you wanted to abolish the Torah and not to fulfill it, you could have done no better than to avoid citing what in fact the Torah says – on which, I gladly concede, you improve in striking ways.

"You tell me a better way to observe some of the Ten Commandments than I knew, but you forgot to tell me that was what you had in mind; you advise me to carry out some of the wise Proverbs, but you do not cite the Proverbs. People are surprised at how you talk, which is not as a master of the Torah but in some other way."

Jesus does not respond to the astonishment of the crowds. With that detail, the account of the great message concludes.

And yet –

And yet I listen in vain, in this message from the mountain, for torah for the people down below, for all of us, all together, equally: Israel. I think what I do not hear troubles more than what I do. For in the end Jesus frames his teaching in a way that wins attention – you have heard it said ..., but I say ..., certainly startles; that is to the good. And much that he says demands respect, some of it assent, and part of the dissent may be mere quibbling.

But if the disciples, standing at the edges of the crowd, came up to me and said, "Not so bad, eh? Come on with us?" I would have said, "If I go with you, I leave God."

And, amazed, they would have said, "How come?"

"Because," I would reply, "when God speaks through Moses, it is to all Israel, but your master speaks to you. The rest of us are outsiders. And God does not know outsiders in Israel, only sinners, whom the Torah teaches to repent.

"Jesus reminds me of a prophet, yes, speaking on his own authority – but not an Israelite prophet. He talks like an outsider, or if he is the insider, then much that he says makes the rest of us outsiders.

"He is one of us, but he sees us from afar, like another prophet on another mountain long ago – but he was a prophet that arose from among the gentiles:

" 'And on the morrow Balak took Balaam and brought him up to Bamoth-baal; and from there he saw the nearest of the people, (Num 22:41).

"For from the top of the mountains I see him, from the hills I behold him", (Num 23:9).

"Seeing always from afar, he came to curse, but was forced by God to bless.

"Your master blesses those who do what he says. Give me, rather, the rebuke of the prophets of Israel than the blessing of the gentiles' prophets.

"His torah is for some of us, but the Torah stands in judgment of us all."

No, if I were there that day, I would not have joined those disciples and followed the master on his way. I would have turned back to my own family and to my village, going on with my life as part of, and within, eternal Israel. Montefiore's explanation says why: "Public justice is outside of his purview" – and so too is that entirety of eternal Israel in which I have my being. I do not mean to give offense. But I do take exception to a teaching that pertains to me personally, but not to my family and my village: to eternal Israel as we here and now embody it.

4

Honor Your Father and Your Mother

vs

Do not Think That I Have Come to Bring Peace on Earth

"Do not think that I have come to bring peace on earth; I have not come to bring peace but a sword. For I have come to set a man against his father, and a daughter against her mother, and a daughter-in-law against her mother-in-law; and a man's foes will be those of his own household. He who loves father or mother more than me is not worthy of me; and he who loves son or daughter more than me is not worthy of me."

Matthew 10:34–37

I t is one thing to decide not to follow the teacher but quietly to go back home, which, after hearing the Sermon on the Mount, I would have done. It is another thing altogether to lose interest in what Jesus had to say. And I cannot imagine, living at that time, I could ever have lost interest. For the same reason that Jesus' teachings conquered and shaped much of world civilization, through the power of the message, not only the might of Christian armies, so even then, no thoughtful person could have heard such challenging words and turned away indifferent. So, heading home, I'd have spent my long afternoon's walk through Galilee reflecting on what I'd heard that day.

With the Torah uppermost in mind, of course, Jesus' striking formulations about the Ten Commandments – not only don't kill, don't get angry; not only don't commit adultery, don't even think about it; not only don't swear falsely ("take the name of the Lord your God in vain"), don't swear at all – would have struck me as his most engaging statements. The reason is not their punctiliousness above the Ten Commandments – don't even come close to breaking them! I would have admired that notion, but hardly thought it fresh; everyone else said to build a fence around the Torah. True, this particular fence extends the border protecting the Commandments from out there to in here: to heart and mind and imagination. True, these sayings touch me in my everyday life, where murder is uncommon, but anger routine; adultery rare, fantasy, always; false swearing exceptional, swearing normal. So he has brought the power of his imagination to bear, and made these commandments immediate and urgent.

But in admiring the power, I reflect also on the pathos, for where we are strong, there is our weakness. To explain what I mean, I point out that we live out our lives not only within, that is, in our conscience. We live also with other people in community. None of us is only an "I," all of us also form parts of a "we." And the "we" is made up of home and family, but also community beyond the walls of our homes. Now, it is clear, Jesus has talked to the private life, just as he spoke of prayer in a closed room. But we, eternal Israel, pray together, not only, or even mainly, on our own, "in a closed room." Jesus' advice runs counter to what and who we are, which is everywhere and always "Israel," a whole people, a community of families, all of us with the same parents and grandparents, Abraham and Sarah, Isaac and Rebecca, Jacob and Leah and Rachel, whose God is the God of us all. That is how we address our prayers to God: "Blessed are you, Lord, our God, God of Abraham, Isaac, and

Jacob ..." How in a closed room is there space for that "we," that whole family?

And that counsel on prayer stands for much more in this torah for the inner life. In fact, the power of the Sermon on the Mount, so far as I can comprehend it, governs one dimension of my existence: the individual. Two other dimensions of human existence – community and family – are sadly omitted. In their natural order, first comes the family, then the village – and only then does the individual find his or her position in the scheme of things. But the first two dimensions of life I thought neglected by the torah I heard from the mountaintop.

But not right away. Impressed by the fresh and profound reading of commandments for the person, only later would my mind have wandered back to my original reservations about Jesus. And I would have cut back to the heart of the issue only when I reviewed in my thought other commandments. Can I read these the way the teacher taught the others? Is there a message I might frame – perhaps not so insistently as "You have heard it said ... but I say to you ..." to be sure – in response to some of the other of the Ten Commandments besides the three he taught with such effect?

I wanted not only to learn lessons but also to draw conclusions, not only to take notes but also to take risks – think beyond what I had heard. For the greatness of this master-teacher lies not only in what he says, but in how he teaches me to think in the way he thinks. And the excellence of a good disciple such as I want to be in this Torah-lesson is shown not by the lessons he learns – but the conclusions he draws. If the good teacher teaches lessons and the good disciple learns them, the great teacher shows how to learn and the great disciple draws conclusions. So, to speak now in the acute present of our own time and my own life, in my life as sometimes-teacher but always-student, sometimes even as disciple of my students of times past, I've learned that a good student takes notes, a great one draws conclusions.

But you draw conclusions only in the setting of putting forth a proposition, suggesting a viewpoint, arguing and challenging, listening attentively to the other and paying attention to what the other says. I take Jesus seriously; even knowing nothing of what will come of his life and teachings, I realize that he puts forth a grand challenge to my grasp of the Torah. So I pay him the tribute of an engaged encounter with his teachings. I want to draw conclusions – and that means to use what I have learned in my own way, to turn imitation into re-formation.

Accordingly the conclusions I wanted to draw, on that long walk home, therefore would concern the right way to think – "You have heard ... but I say to you ..." – and then that wonderful "fence for the Torah" announced in such challenging, insistent language. In my mind I think of a match for the three commandments of personal conduct – not to murder, not to commit adultery, not to take the name of the Lord my God in vain. As I work through the Commandments, I look for those that tell me how to live my life. So I pass by the great theological commandments that form the prologue: not to have other gods, not to make a graven image.

But what about the space between very public, and intensely personal: not all Israel in the abstract, under the aspect of Heaven's perspective, but also not private life, prayer in the closed room, all by myself. Here we are in the middle, where life is lived, with people: Israel in community. The family, the building block of the social order?

Jesus begins with fundamental affirmations about life with God. He concludes with teachings about the personal life. In the middle, between the opening, theological commandments and the closing, personal ones, I find two commandments, both of them focused on life in community: that is, on the society of the here and the now. That is where I live; that is where life flourishes; so these attract my attention:

Remember the sabbath day, to keep it holy. Six days you shall labor, and do all your work; but the seventh day is a sabbath to the Lord your God; in it you shall not do any work, you, or your son, or your daughter, your manservant, or your maidservant, or your cattle, or the sojourner who is within your gates; for in six days the Lord made heaven and earth, the sea, and all that is in them, and rested the seventh day; therefore the Lord blessed the sabbath day and hallowed it. (Exod 20:8–11)

Honor your father and your mother, that your days may be long in the land which the Lord your God gives you. (Exod 20:12)

Here we deal not with God and the people, Israel, on the one side, or with the conduct of individuals, matters of right action and (Jesus rightly insists – and among teachers of torah, he is not alone) right thought as well, on the other.

One commandment concerns the Sabbath with reference to creation; the other, the home and family in particular: the household. Here I reflect not upon all Israel, on the one side, or my own conduct, on the other, but the building block of eternal Israel from Abraham, Isaac, and Jacob down to my mother and my father. In the coming chapter, I'll try to spell out the commandment concerning the Sabbath, the moment at which the family and home become sealed with other families and homes for a sacred moment into a single place, and in which that sacred space celebrates the creation of the natural world: the sanctification of space and place in nature. And – to come right to the point – Jesus' teaching about the commandment concerning the family – "Honor your father and your mother, that your days may be long in the land which the Lord your God gives you" (Exod 20:12) – startles and alarms me. He directly contradicts the Torah when he says, "I have come to set a man against his father, and a daughter against her mother ..."

Eternal Israel holds the land – so the Ten Commandments say – in virtue of honor of father and mother. When God says to Moses, "… that your days may be long in the land which the Lord your God gives you," the stakes are not trivial. Now, in the context of Jesus' own message, a disciple may point out to me that to follow Jesus, I have to place his call above even my love for parents: "… he who does not take his cross and follow me is not worthy of me. He who finds his life will lose it, and he who loses his life for my sake will find it" (Matt 10:38–39). And yet, if I do what he says, I abandon my father and my mother, my brothers and sisters, my wife and my children. Then what is to be of Israel? For if all of us do what he wants, then the family disintegrates, the home collapses, and what holds the village and the land together, the body of the family, gives way. To follow him, do I have to violate one of the Ten Commandments?

Not only so, but in the representation of the Torah, "Israel" forms a family: that is to say, "Israel" here and now,"Israel after the flesh," in later Christian language, the actual, living, present family of Abraham and Sarah, Isaac and Rebecca, Jacob and Leah and Rachel. We pray to the God we know, to begin with, through the testimony of our family, to the God of Abraham and Sarah, Isaac and Rebecca, Jacob and Leah and Rachel. So to explain who we are, eternal Israel, sages appeal to the metaphor of genealogy, because to begin with, they point to the fleshly connection, the family, as the rationale for Israel's social existence. And Jesus would do the same, turning the metaphor on its head: my family is made up of people who do what God wants, turning genealogy into the effect of true piety.

That is why I call the commandment concerning the honor due to father and to mother not personal and private, but public, social, and corporate. And Jesus calls into question the primacy of the family in the priority of my responsibilities, the centrality of the family in the social order. Not only so, but Jesus says so explicitly:

While he was still speaking to the people, behold, his mother and his brothers stood outside, asking to speak to him. But he replied to the man who told him, "Who is my mother, and who are my brothers?" And stretching out his hand toward his disciples, he said, "Here are my mother and my brothers! For whoever does the will of my Father in heaven is my brother, and sister, and mother." (Matt 12:46–50)

Does Jesus not teach me to violate one of the two great commandments of the Ten Commandments that concern the social order?

The disciple may argue, "But to serve him, we have to go with him. The father and the mother give life in this world; Jesus, whom we know as Christ, gives life eternal." And even in a more homely, academic framework – for we are able to deal only with Jesus' teachings, with Jesus as a teacher of specific propositions – the way to learn is to follow, to imitate, to observe. It is to listen and discuss – not merely to stand at the foot of a mountain for an hour or so. So the disciple – Matthew himself perhaps? – would conclude: "Just standing around for an hour is not to learn his torah, it is only to hear his words."

How, after all, is any master going to teach true lessons, except by example, gesture more than word? The Torah left as a mere book dies, mere words on a page or a parchment. The Torah comes to life, in particular, in attitude and action, in the way in which masters of the Torah embody it. So the demand to study the Torah at some point is going to conflict with the requirement to honor father and mother. Not only so, but after all, Jesus' disciples even now neglect not only their parents but family duties. And if a disciple is married, then what is to come of wife and children? The Torah commands us not only to honor parents but also to carry out our responsibilities to our spouse: what of that?

In a world in which it is taken for granted that disciples and masters are all men, what is to become of the wives? So at stake is more than parents, it is the wife and children, the home – the entire household, described with such detail in the commandment

on the Sabbath, "you, or your son, or your daughter, your manservant, or your maidservant, or your cattle, or the sojourner who
is within your gates" (Exod 20:10). What troubles me deeply,
therefore, is that if I follow Jesus, I abandon my home and family,
but the Torah has conferred upon me sacred duties to home and
family – and community too. Does Jesus not affirm that it is our
task to carry out the commandment that God gave even to Adam
and Eve: to be fruitful and multiply, to perpetuate life on earth?
Matthew does not tell us that he has married or has a family of
his own children; and he does tell his disciples to take up the
cross and follow him; and yet, fundamental to the kingdom of
Heaven that the Torah asks eternal Israel to bring about is the formation of an enduring society in sanctification.

The same issue faced the Torah's masters and disciples later on,
and after all, that prescient disciple will point out, in time to come
masters would call disciples away from home and family, and
they would leave their wives and children for long periods of
time, so as to study the Torah. Indeed, one of the great love stories of Judaism builds on precisely that motif: the willingness of
the wife to send her husband to study the Torah, even to the neglect of herself. So what Jesus asks for himself is no more than
what the masters of the Torah asked for the Torah: place that
above home and family:

> Rabbi Aqiba was the [unlettered] shepherd of Ben Kalba Sabua. His
> daughter saw that he was chaste and noble. She said to him, "If we be-
> come betrothed to you, will you go to the school house?"
> He said to her, "Yes."
> She became betrothed to him secretly and sent him off.
> Her father heard and drove her out of his house and forbade her by
> vow from enjoying his property.
> He went and remained at the session for twelve years at the school
> house. When he came back, he brought with him twelve thousand disci-

ples. He heard a sage say to her, "How long are you going to lead the life of a life-long widow?"

She said to him, "If he should pay attention to what I want, he will spend another twelve years in study."

He said, "So what I'm doing is with [her] permission." He went back and stayed in session another twelve years at the school house.

When he came back, he brought with him twenty-four thousand disciples. His wife heard and went out to meet him. Her neighbors said to her, "Borrow some nice clothes and put them on."

She said to them, "'A righteous man will recognize the soul of his cattle' (Prov 12:10)."

When she came to him, she fell on his face and kissed his feet. His attendants were going to push her away. He said to them, "Leave her alone! What is mine and what is yours is entirely hers."

Her father heard that an eminent authority had come to town. He said, "I shall go to him. Maybe he'll release me from my vow." He came to him. He said to him, "Did you take your vow with an eminent authority in mind [as your son-in-law]?"

He said to him, "Even if he had known a single chapter, even if he had known a single law [I would never have taken that vow]!"

He said to him, "I am the man."

He fell on his face and kissed his feet and gave him half of his property.
(Babylonian Talmud Tractate Ketubot 62B-63A)

So why take issue with Jesus for telling disciples, "He who loves father or mother more than me is not worthy of me; and he who loves son or daughter more than me is not worthy of me"? If the Torah were personified – as Wisdom is personified in Scripture – it could have said no less. All Jesus asked was that disciples place their love of him over their love of family. And is he not forming a family built on the intangible beams of loyalty and love – a supernatural family, in that love in the end resonates what is beyond the merely natural? And is that not also a family, indeed the building block of the kingdom of Heaven, the new house of Israel? So the disciple might say in the master's behalf.

Not only so but, the prescient disciple might well observe, other masters later on would require no less – and here, too, the disciple is right. In the Torah as it would be interpreted by other sages, Israel would be instructed to place honor for the Torah, in the person of the sage, even above honor for the father and the mother. How different is such an instruction from the one that Jesus has given in his own behalf? In a moment we shall turn to the sole point of difference, which is, of course, the contrast: Torah as against Christ. In the formulation of sages later on, we find precisely the same contrast that we drew in Jesus' behalf: genealogy against another bond, besides the one of family, a supernatural tie, in an exact sense of the word, "a holy family," a family founded on holiness, on love that surpasses understanding – in secular, descriptive terms, on supernatural love. No wonder Roman Catholic and Orthodox Christianity would find themselves so much at home in the arms of the Virgin Mary, to use their language in their context.

In what follows, first of all, learning in the Torah is contrasted with genealogical status, a matter important to Israel in that time. Therefore while the castes of the Temple, the priests and Levites, took precedence, and while these castes derived their status from their genealogy – going back to Aaron and Moses, respectively, so the Torah said – nonetheless, a disciple of a sage took precedence. Thus:

> A priest takes precedence over a Levite, a Levite over an Israelite, an Israelite over a person whose parents were not legally permitted to marry ...
> Under what circumstances?
> When all of them are equivalent.
> But if the person whose parents were not legally permitted to marry was a disciple of a sage and a high priest was an unlettered person, then

the person whose parents were not legally permitted to marry who is a disciple of a sage takes precedence over a high priest who is an unlettered person. (Mishnah-tractate Horayot 3:8)

Since a person whose parents were not legally permitted to marry (e.g., brother and sister, among various possibilities) bequeathed a most difficult genealogical, and also (by the way) social, status, the statement that such a person took precedence over a high priest represents a considerable claim. In our own context, the statement is like saying that a lowly assistant professor of political science takes precedence at a state dinner over the President not of his university but of the United States of America – and we still could not grasp the radical character of this statement. For the daughter of the President (University, United States) may marry an assistant professor or even a graduate student; but the daughter of a Priest would never, never, ever marry the offspring of an illegitimate union.

Now that is the power of the statement, "But if the person whose parents were not legally permitted to marry was a disciple of a sage and a high priest was an unlettered person, then the person whose parents were not legally permitted to marry who is a disciple of a sage takes precedence over a high priest who is an unlettered person." So if what Jesus meant to say was that his call is meant to take precedence over all other callings, then, in the context that would surface later on, I could well identify his call with the Torah's teaching as I understood it. That is to say, the lowliest disciple of the master took precedence over the most distinguished family heritage.

The Torah then takes the place of genealogy, and the master of Torah gains a new lineage. In that context, I can well understand how, in his setting, Jesus as my master is supposed to provide me with what one might call a new lineage. He is comparable to a father, a spiritual one to be sure. In that context, can I accommodate myself to his claim to identify a new family, a family formed in response to the fatherhood of God and discipleship to Jesus: "Here are my mother and my brothers! For whoever does the will of my Father in heaven is my brother and sister and mother." Can I make sense of such a statement in terms of the Torah as I understand it now? Yes, without difficulty.

And yet – it is precisely at that point in the unfolding of the argument that in time to come I should have to take issue. For as discipleship would play itself out in the minds of other sages of the Torah besides Jesus, matters are hardly so simple. It would not be said that the disciple has to reject the father in favor of the new father, the master, even though the father has brought the son into this world, while the master would bring him into the life of the world to come. What would be said is quite different: the master takes precedence over the father; but the father and the master and the disciple remain bound into a single bond, a social order that endures. For example:

> [If he has to choose between seeking] what he has lost and what his father has lost, his own takes precedence. [If he has to choose between seeking] what he has lost and what his master has lost, his own takes precedence. [If he has to choose between seeking] what his father has lost and what his master has lost, that of his master takes precedence. For his father brought him into this world. But his master, who taught him wisdom, will bring him into the life of the world to come. But if his father is a sage, that of his father takes precedence. [If] his father and his master were carrying heavy burdens, he removes that of his master, and afterward removes that of his father. [If] his father and his master were taken captive, he ransoms his master, and afterward he ransoms his father. But if his father is a sage, he ransoms his father, and afterward he ransoms his master. (Mishnah-tractate Baba Mesia 2:11)

To begin with, one is responsible for oneself. But what is striking here is, first, that the master and the father compete – but only if the latter is not a master of the Torah; if he is, then the master who teaches the Torah does not take precedence over the father who enjoys the same status.

Here the analogy I just offered – Christ takes precedence over the family (supernatural relationship over natural genealogy), just as the Torah takes priority over the family – fails, because it is slightly out of focus. For the sages represented by the rules at hand, the Torah brings about the equality of all Israel (then: males; nowadays, men and women alike). If there is a relationship of two different but comparable claims – the sage as against the unlettered parent – then the superiority rests in knowledge of the Torah. But if there is a relationship of two equal claims – the sages as against the father who also is a sage – then the claim of the father, based on both Torah and genealogy, outweighs the claim of the sage.

In the setting of that exposition, the original analogy seems somewhat blurred and out of focus. I compared Christ and Torah, but that comparison seems awry. For the focus is neither the master nor the father, but the Torah. How so? It is knowledge of the Torah that endows either man with standing; but if both of them enjoy the same standing, then the father takes precedence. Can Jesus' saying be read in an analogous manner? In no way, because the discipleship to Christ is unique. It is not discipleship to the Torah, which anyone may master, that will endow with supernatural status the relationship of any two persons, master and disciple. It is discipleship to Jesus Christ, uniquely, that is at issue, and to that standing, the standing of Christ, only Jesus is called. "Whoever does the will of my Father in heaven is my brother and sister" is simply not the same thing as "whoever becomes a sage, master of the Torah, enters into the standing of the Torah." The one is particular, specific to Jesus, the other general, applicable to anyone. The Torah stands in one world, Christ in another.

So here again we observe how deeply personal is the focus of Jesus' teaching: it is on himself, not on his message. We realize full well that anyone may master the Torah and share in the same

status; but Jesus is the only model: "Take up your cross and follow me" is not the same thing as "study the Torah that I teach,
which I have studied from my master before me." "Follow me"
and "follow the Torah" look alike, but they are not alike. They
are, indeed, quite the opposite. Any (in that time, male; but today,
female or male) Israelite can master the Torah and become a sage,
but only Jesus can be Jesus Christ.

Nothing in the analogy I have drawn between one mode –
Jesus' – and another mode – the Mishnah's, as cited above – of
discipleship to a sage, prepares me for that claim, which falls far
beyond the boundaries of the Torah, which is in the end simply
not relevant to the Torah. To argue that in telling me that I cannot
love my mother and my father more than I love him, Jesus is telling me to violate one of the Ten Commandments proves, really,
irrelevant: that is not what is at stake. What I have done to this
point is only undertake a comparison that has yielded a stunning
contrast. But arguments are not formed on the basis of demon-
strations that parallel lines don't meet. So how am I to offer my
argument with Jesus, in that time, in that place, formed around
the issues that all of us have to work out everywhere and always?

For that argument, we have to define an issue in which what is
at stake has nothing to do with the Torah, but rather with what we
owe to God. What is God's stake in honoring mother and father?
Jesus is very clear on this point in the same passage: "He who receives you receives me, and he who receives me receives him who
sent me" (Matt 10:40). So at stake is not only honor of father and
mother as against honor of the master, nor is it merely whether or
not we can go so far as to neglect parents in favor of following
Jesus (or studying the Torah). Here we find a claim, in connection
with honor of father and mother, equivalent to the claim of Jesus:

Rabbi [Judah the Patriarch] says, "Precious before the One who spoke
and brought the world into being is the honor owing to father and
mother,

"for he has declared equal the honor owing to them and the honor owing to him, the fear owing to them and the fear owing to him, cursing them and cursing him.

"It is written: Honor your father and your mother," and as a counterpart: 'Honor the Lord with your substance' (Prov 3:9).

"Scripture thus has declared equal the honor owing to them and the honor owing to him.

" 'You shall fear every man his mother and his father' (Lev 19:3), and, as a counterpart: 'You shall fear the Lord your God' (Deut 6:13).

"Scripture thus has declared equal the fear owing to them and the fear owing to him.

" 'And he who curses his father or his mother shall surely be put to death' (Exod 21:17), and correspondingly: 'Whoever curses his God' (Lev 24:15).

"Scripture thus has declared equal the cursing them and cursing him."

[Rabbi continues,] "Come and note that the reward [for obeying the two commandments is the same].

" 'Honor the Lord with your substance ... so shall your barns be filled with plenty' (Prov 3:9–10), and 'Honor your father and your mother that your days may be long in the land which the Lord your God gives you.'

" 'You shall fear the Lord your God' (Deut 6:13), as a reward: 'But to you that fear my name shall the sun of righteousness arise with healing in its wings' (Mal 3:20).

" 'You shall fear every man his mother and his father and you shall keep my sabbaths' (Lev 19:3).

"And as a reward? 'If you turn away your foot because of the Sabbath, then you shall delight yourself in the Lord' (Isa 58:13–14)." (Mekhilta Attributed to Rabbi Ishmael Bahodesh 8 [trans. J. Neusner: 54:3–5])

Now we see what is truly at stake: honor of parents forms a this-worldly analogy to honor of God. So the issue is not discipleship alone, but the comparison between and among relationships: relationship of disciple to master, relationship of child to parent, relationship of human being to God. And that brings me back to that argument I should have wanted to conduct with, if not Jesus that day, then his disciple the next day: "And is your master God?" For, I now realize, only God can demand of me what Jesus is asking.

So if, with the disciple, I cannot reply, "Yes, in following Jesus I follow God," if I cannot do that, then I also cannot follow that master along the path that he by his own words sets before me. In the end the master, Jesus, makes a demand that only God makes – as the later patriarch of Israel, Judah, at the end of the second century, would spell matters out in what would be assigned to him in a still-later piece of writing. Jesus' link of family to master-disciple-circle forms only the first step, leading not to honor of the master like, or more than, honor of the parent, but, ultimately, honor of the master like, or as much as, honor of God.

Earlier, I observed that some want to draw a line between the "Jesus of history" and the "Christ of faith," or distinguish the faith of Jesus from the faith of Paul, or separate Jesus Christ from the Christian Church, his mystical body. Some Christians maintain that the historical Jesus, the man who really lived and taught, would not have recognized the faith that the Christian Church formulated later on. They identify with the "authentic" teachings of Jesus the man, but not with the added-on doctrines in the name of Christ, formulated, they allege, by the Church.

Not only so, but Jewish critics of Christianity distinguish between Jesus, whom they honor as a rabbi or even a great prophet by reason of the nobility of his teachings, and Christianity; they portray Jesus as a Galilean wonder-worker or rabbi or prophet, but not as Christ. There are scholars, both Christian and Jewish, who draw a line between the Jesus whom they admire, and the apostle, Paul, whom, they allege, changed the faith of Jesus the rabbi or prophet into the religion of Christ. In all, both Judaic and Christian reading of the New Testament yields a distinction important in its own terms and context.

Since I want to argue only within the framework of a single Gospel and that evangelist's story about Jesus and sayings in Jesus' name, I obviously cannot enter into the discussion of these much more complicated questions. But I have to ask myself why we cannot identify in the sayings of Matthew's Jesus not only the Jesus of history but also the Christ of faith. The distinction between the one and the other, important for some forms of Christianity and for some theologians and apologists for both Judaism and Christianity, strikes me as not well founded.

For if people in general do accept that Jesus really said the sayings we are now seeing, then we have to put forth some second thoughts about distinguishing between Jesus of history and Christ of faith. For in these observations about what is at stake in a very humble matter, honor of parents as against "He who loves father or mother more than me is not worthy of me," I find myself unable to recognize that abyss between the man, Jesus, and the Christ of faith. Jesus makes sense, as we have seen, only in the setting of the Christ of faith. When we compare what he says on the commandment to honor parents with what other sages have to say, indeed, when we find our way to an appropriate comparison – one in which each side of the equation really does correspond to the other – we see in the Jesus of history precisely that Christ of faith that, for twenty centuries, Christians have found as much in Matthew's Jesus as in Paul's Christ.

Then where do we find that promised argument, the one I should like to present to Jesus the man? If, in all earnestness, I could speak a few words with Jesus the sage, I still should want to know: "Then master, what of Israel in its families and villages? Do you have a torah to teach us who love our fathers and our mothers, our sons and our daughters? And we, the householders in our homes, we who form in the here and the now that eternal Israel that stands forever before Sinai's Torah – what of us?"

What marks the master is the power to listen to the disciple: to answer the question that is asked, not the one the master wants to answer, and these are never the same. So the true sage (and it is not condescending to say that, in the Gospel narratives throughout, Jesus provides a model for the teacher), will ask a question to clarify the question (and maybe answer it too). So Jesus may want to know, "What do you mean, what of us?"

And I will now say what is on my mind, rather than asking him to read it: "I grasp your teaching on not murdering, not committing adultery, not taking false oaths. Your fence around those Commandments of the Torah stands tall and firm. I am a better person because I heard your torah, truer to God's Torah than I could have been before: you really did fulfill, clarify, elaborate; you in no way abolish or destroy.

"But then, is everything in your torah's fulfillment of the Torah to speak only to my conduct as one person? Is there no torah for me as part of a family, as part of that Israel that existed before Sinai and assembled at the foot of Sinai: children of Abraham and Sarah, Isaac and Rebecca, Jacob and Leah and Rachel? I am of the family of Israel. What have you to say to me in that family?"

It is presumptuous of me to ask the master to repeat something he may already have said. So before going on, I think through this teaching I have heard, this Sermon on the Mount. In quest for a message to the families that make up the family of Israel, I look for a message in that sermon, specifically, in what Matthew at chapters 5 through 7 reports Jesus said that day. Is there something that pertains not to "all Israel" in relationship to God – "You shall have no other gods before me" – nor to me personally in relationship to God, but to me as part of my family, that basic building block of Israel's social order?

The answer, of course, will come from the identification of that "you" to whom Jesus did speak on the mountain. That it is "me personally" I take for granted; but "you" is plural, not only singular, and before Jesus were many "me"s. And to know whom he meant by his "you," we have to juggle the two audiences: "and when he sat down his disciples came to him. And he opened his mouth and taught them saying ..." (Matt 5:1–2). So there is the audience of the disciples, at the top of the hill, and there is the mass of Israel, at the bottom.

"Master, who is your 'you'? The disciples only? Obviously not. Much that you said that day spoke to all of us. Then all of us in general? Certainly not. Some of the things pertain to your disciples in particular: 'Blessed are you when men revile you and persecute you and utter all kinds of evil against you falsely on my account' (Matt. 5:11) for example, among many examples.

"Master, is there an Israel in your 'You?' – not an 'Israel' out there, in the abstract, but an 'Israel' in here, in my village, in my family?

"Master, do you speak only to me, not to my family? only to your family of disciples, not to your family after the flesh?

"So, master, where is there place, and space, in your 'you' for that 'us' that make up Israel?"

The master does not have to answer that question. He already has. He has other things in mind. I am asking my questions; he is giving his answers. Unless I ask his questions, I am not going to hear his answers. In his answers, I hear a reply to my questions too:

"Therefore I tell you, do not be anxious about your life, what you shall eat or what you shall drink, nor about your body, what you shall put on. Is not life more than food, and the body more than clothing? Look at the birds of the air; they neither sow nor reap nor gather into barns, and yet your heavenly Father feeds them. Are you not of more value than they? And which of you by being anxious can add one cubit to his span of life? ... do not be anxious, saying, 'What shall we eat?' or 'What shall we drink?' or 'What shall we wear? For the Gentiles seek all these things; and your heavenly Father knows that you need them all. But seek first his kingdom and his righteousness, and all these things shall be yours as well." (Matt 6:25–27, 31–33)

Here the master clearly means to speak to Israel with a "you" that includes us all. He is explicit, when he contrasts this "you"

71

with the Gentiles; so the gentiles seek these things, but "your heavenly Father" knows you need them. So Jesus does have a message to me in Israel. But the Israel here is not family and village; the concerns of family and village, that Israel of the here and now, for food and drink and clothing and shelter – these God of course will attend to. But then, if what should concern me is his kingdom and his righteousness, where I live, with whom I live – these really bear no consequence. Once more, we find a message in the silence, as much as in the speech, we hear from the top of the mountain. This "Israel" is then something other than, different from, that Israel of home and family that I know. And my argument consists in only one "but":

"But, Sir, the Israel of home and family is where I am."

And that leads me to ask my other question provoked by my reckoning with the Ten Commandments: *What of Israel where it is, what of Israel when it takes place?* And to clarify these somewhat opaque questions and spell out why they matter, we turn to the one of the Ten Commandments that tells us to sanctify the Sabbath, the commandment that speaks of time and space: Israel in the here and now of home and village.

5

Remember the Sabbath Day to Keep It Holy

vs

Look, Your Disciples Are Doing What Is Not Lawful to Do on the Sabbath

At that time Jesus went through the grainfields on the sabbath; his disciples were hungry, and they began to pluck ears of grain and to eat. But when the Pharisees saw it, they said to him, "Look, your disciples are doing what is not lawful to do on the Sabbath. He said to them, "Have you not read what David did, when he was hungry and those who were with him: how he entered the house of God and ate the bread of the Presence, which it was not lawful for him to eat nor for those who were with him, but only for the priests? Or have you not read in the law how on the Sabbath the priests in the temple profane the Sabbath, and are guiltless? I tell you, something greater than the temple is here. And if you had known what this means, 'I desire mercy and not sacrifice [Hos. 6:6],' you would not have condemned the guiltless. For the Son of man is lord of the Sabbath."

Matthew 12:1–8

The master's many miracles – healing leprosy, paralysis, and fever; calming the storm; driving out demons – stories about such wonders will have caught my attention. But

I would have been used to wonders; the Torah made me expect them, and wonder-workers even then would not have disappointed me. Such things may have been necessary, but to me were trivial. For my concern would have lain not in finding supernatural proofs for the master's propositions, but in learning from him what he had to teach me about the Torah: analysis, argument, evidence. And to Jesus' own credit, he dismissed people who kept demanding a sign; what mattered was the message.

So as the master made his way through the towns and villages, teaching in "their" synagogues, "preaching the gospel of the kingdom, healing every disease and every infirmity" (Matt 9:35), I should have taken a position of friendly, patient interest. And anyhow, the talk I'd heard him give at the mountain in Galilee left me filled with thought.

With the Ten Commandments still in mind, though, I should have paid more than routine attention to what the master did and said on the Sabbath. For, in the everyday life of the Torah, the Sabbath marked the climax and fulfillment. Remembering the Sabbath day to keep it holy formed, and now forms, what eternal Israel does together: it is what makes eternal Israel what it is, the people that, like God in creating the world, rest from creation on the Seventh Day. The Sabbath has both positive and negative sides; on that day, we do not do servile work. On that day, we do celebrate creation. For six days we make things; on the seventh, we appreciate them.

True, watching what the master and the disciples do or don't do the Sabbath and judging them on that account would open me to the charge of being "holier than thou." Who am I to supervise someone else's life of sanctification? God cares for us all – but God alone stands in judgment of us all. It is not the sort of issue I would have wanted to raise. But if Jesus raised it, or if his disciples acted in a way that people in general found surprising and troubling, that would be another matter. And that is how things would work out. There would not be even a pretense of keeping the Sabbath in the way that people ordinarily did.

Well, why would it matter so much? Is the Torah just a collection of hocus pocus, of do's and don'ts? Not at all. The stakes for the Sabbath are very high, and that is precisely why Jesus and his disciples would set forth their doctrine, also, in the setting of Sabbath-life and holiness. For not working on the Sabbath stands for more than nitpicking ritual. It is a way of imitating God. God rested on the Sabbath day and declared the Sabbath day holy (Gen 2:1–4). And that explains why we who form eternal Israel rest on the Sabbath day, enjoy it, make it a holy day. We do on the Seventh Day what God did on the Seventh Day of creation.

And that makes all the more striking Jesus' presentation of the matter. In choosing the Sabbath as a point of issue, he identifies a critical issue, rather than just going around doing wonders and marvels without a message or a meaning to convey. In particular, and of greatest interest, Jesus treats the Sabbath in two statements, which stand side by side. The two statements, appropriately, deal with the Sabbath first in the setting of our relationship with God, and only second, in the context of the things we do, and do not do, on that particular day. So Jesus stands well within the framework of the Torah in his presentation of what he wishes to say about the Sabbath: a this-worldly moment that bespeaks eternity. The Sabbath forms the centerpiece of our life with God, and Jesus treats it as the centerpiece of his teaching; only as a second thought do the do's and don'ts matter.

These statements on the Sabbath (as Matthew tells me about them) appropriately stand in close sequence. First Jesus speaks about rest from work, and then, and only then, about the Sabbath. Putting the two together we find a remarkable message:

All things have been delivered to me by my Father; and no one knows the Son except the Father, and no one knows the Father except the Son and any one to whom the Son chooses to reveal him. Come to me, all who labor and are heavy-laden, and I will give you rest. Take my yoke upon you, and learn from me; for I am gentle and lowly in heart, and you will find rest for your souls. For my yoke is easy and my burden is light. (Matt 11:27–30)

Since, on the Sabbath, I rest as God rested on the Seventh Day of creation, I find entirely appropriate the focus here: how do I come to God? And how do I find rest?

These two questions in any other context but that of the Torah will appear disconnected. But the Ten Commandments include the one that says, "Remember the sabbath day, to keep it holy … for in six days the Lord made heaven and earth, the sea, and all that is in them, and rested on the seventh day; therefore the Lord blessed the sabbath day and hallowed it." Now, when we remember that we keep the Sabbath because God rested on the Sabbath, we realize that keeping the Sabbath makes us like God. Then the theme of labor and heavy burdens, on the one side, rest on the other, forms a close fit with, "Come to me, and I will give you rest."

Standing by itself, Jesus' statement speaks only about rest. But as we see, in the very same context, he speaks of the Sabbath. So, hearing what he said, I think only of the Sabbath, which is how eternal Israel finds rest for its soul: "Six days you shall labor, and do all your work; but the seventh day is a sabbath to the Lord your God; in it you shall not do any work" (Exod 20:9–10). The issue is not trivial and not to be treated as a matter of some silly ritual, like not stepping on the cracks in the sidewalks. The stakes are very high.

God told us through Isaiah, "If you … call the sabbath a delight … if you honor it, not going your own ways, or seeking your own pleasure, or talking idly; then you shall take delight in the Lord …" (Isa 58:13–14). When I hear about rest for my soul, surcease for my labor, Jesus speaks of exchanging my heavy burden for his and so finding rest. And in that same context, I learn, in Matthew's report, about how Jesus' disciples picked food on the Sabbath – Isaiah might have called this "seeking your own pleasure," or "going about your own ways" (Isa 58:13) – and how he explained who's who and what's what: "the Son of man is lord of the sabbath."

This teaching stands alongside an action, that "it is lawful to do good on the Sabbath":

> And he went on from there, and entered their synagogue. And behold, there was a man with a withered hand. And they asked him, "Is it lawful to heal on the sabbath?" so that they might accuse him. He said to them, "What man of you, if he has one sheep and it falls into a pit on the sabbath, will not lay hold of it and lift it out? Of how much more value is a man than a sheep! So it is lawful to do good on the sabbath." (Matt 12:9–12)

But, we see, at issue in the Sabbath is not a question of ethics ("it is lawful to do good"). Now when we remember why we rest on the Sabbath, we must find somewhat jarring the allegation, "It is lawful to do good on the Sabbath." The reason is that that statement is simply beside the point; the Sabbath is not about doing good or not doing good; the issue of the Sabbath is holiness, and in the Torah, to be holy is to be like God.

To be sure, the commandment on the Sabbath is explicit, giving two distinct, equally valid accounts of the Sabbath:

> For in six days the Lord made heaven and earth, the sea, and all that is in them and rested on the Seventh day; therefore the Lord blessed the sabbath day and hallowed it. (Exod 20:11)

> Observe the sabbath day to keep it holy ... You shall remember that you were a servant in the land of Egypt, and the Lord your God brought you out thence with a mighty hand and an outstretched arm; therefore the Lord your God commanded you to keep the sabbath day. (Deut 5:12, 15)

The Sabbath celebrates creation: I rest on that day from my creation because God rested on that day in creating the world; I rest on that day to remember I am not a slave, and my slave rests that day too, to be reminded that the slave is not a slave. In both aspects, the Sabbath imposes itself upon the social order, the defining moment of society, in particular a social order that organizes itself around the days of the week.

In addressing the issue of the Sabbath, therefore, Jesus and his disciples strike squarely at the critical issue: What do we do to imitate God? How do we so live as to make ourselves into that "eternal Israel" that God through the Torah has brought into being? Like the honor owing to father and mother, therefore, the celebration of the Sabbath defines what makes Israel Israel. The entire way of life of the community centers on that day. Here is an example of how every moment of the week points toward that one holy day:

> Eleazar ben Hananiah ben Hezekiah ben Garon says, "'Remember the Sabbath day to keep it holy: '
>
> "You should remember it from Sunday, so that if something nice comes to hand, you should set it aside for the sake of the Sabbath."
>
> Rabbi Isaac says, "You should not count the days of the week the way others do, but rather, you should count for the sake of the Sabbath [the first day, the second day, upward to the seventh which is the Sabbath]."
> (Mekhilta Attributed to Rabbi Ishmael LIII:II.7)

The first point is that the six working days point toward the Seventh Day, and throughout the week, we are to remember the Sabbath, even counting the days toward the seventh. How then are we to celebrate the Sabbath? It is in attitude of mind: to give ourselves release from the very thought of work:

> "Six days you shall labor and do all your work:"
> But can a mortal carry out all of one's work in only six days?
> But the nature of Sabbath rest is such that it should be as though all of your labor has been carried out.
> Another teaching [as to "Six days you shall labor and do all your work:"]

"Take a Sabbath rest from the very thought of work."

And so Scripture says, "If you turn away your foot because of the Sabbath" (Isa 58:13), and then, "Then you shall delight yourself in the Lord" (Isa 58:14). (Mekhilta Attributed to Rabbi Ishmael LIII:II.9, 10)

No one completes the work of creation in six days; even God's work of creation goes on continually. That then is not the point of the Sabbath. What is the point is that, on that day, we think not about creation but about celebration of creation: a day of appreciation. And the concluding line is the key: If you turn away from work on the Sabbath, then you have delight in God. So, once more, we appreciate that the Sabbath is our way of taking delight in God. And not surprisingly, the Sabbath is God's gift to humanity, since God did not need the rest, but we do:

"and rested on the seventh day:"

And does fatigue affect God? Is it not said, "The creator of the ends of the earth does not faint and is not weary" (Isa 40:28), "He gives power to the faint" (Isa 40:29); "By the word of the Lord the heavens were made" (Ps 33:6)?

How then can Scripture say, "and rested on the seventh day"?

It is as if [God] had it written concerning himself that he created the world in six days and rested on the seventh.

Now you may reason *a fortiori*:

Now if the One who is not affected by fatigue had it written concerning himself that he created the world in six days and rested on the seventh, how much the more so should a human being, concerning whom it is written, "but man is born to trouble" (Job 5: 7) [also rest on the Sabbath]? (Mekhilta Attributed to Rabbi Ishmael LIII:II.17)

In all of these statements, we gain a grasp of the issues of the Sabbath Day, and in that context, we see that heaven and earth meet on the Sabbath; God and humanity join together, with humanity imitating God in a very concrete and specific way.

The social order of eternal Israel takes shape not in the division of time alone. It concerns also the delineation of space, for society becomes concrete both in time and in place. When, therefore, we see the Sabbath as the defining moment in the life of eternal Israel, we anticipate that that statement tells only part of the tale. The other part concerns where Israel locates itself, and not only when the Sabbath takes over to sanctify Israel. The definition of where Israel is to be found receives a concrete definition on the Sabbath, because of a simple rule of the Torah.

God told Moses to tell the people to stay home on the Seventh Day: "'See! The Lord has given you the sabbath, therefore on the sixth day he gives you bread for two days; remain every man of you in his place, let no one go out of his place on the seventh day. So the people rested on the seventh day" (Exod 16:29–30). So to keep the Sabbath, one remains at home. It is not enough merely not to work. One also has to rest. And resting means, re-forming one day a week the circle of family and household, everyone at home and in place; reentering the life of village and community, no matter how life is lived on the other six days of creation. I myself can understand this deep concern for place, which the advent of the holy day – sacred time – elicits. When my children were growing up, I made it my primary commitment always to be with them on the Sabbath, for Friday night supper, when we gathered as a family. I brought into my home my students, to make them part of my family, and to extend my children's conception of what a family is. It is the Sabbath that makes of the Jewish family a holy family, and it is by remaining at home and within even the physical limits of the home that the family in the here and now of concrete, everyday life, is realized: made real.

So we're not dealing here with hocus pocus, some magical line we're not supposed to cross. We're dealing with the interplay of time and space on an enchanted day: the day that turns us into something other than what we think we are. In the context of the cited verse, which tells people not to go out into the fields on the Sabbath to collect manna, it follows that people are not supposed to carry burdens from place to place. They are supposed to stay home, and they also are supposed not to transport things from place to place: two sides to the same coin. What I understand is that I am not to labor on the Sabbath, I am not to gather food or carry burdens. But by contrast, I remain in my place. What it means to "remain in my place" is that I am to enjoy the rest in my own village.

The prohibition against carrying or moving objects around from one place to another on the Sabbath Day takes effect at the advent of the Sabbath, which marks the end of the time of bearing burdens. In this law of the Torah, therefore, we are told about a day that defines Israel in time and in place. Accordingly, the Torah lays the foundations for the construction of the holy life of eternal Israel on the Sabbath Day. Exodus 16:29–30 require each person to stay where he is on the Seventh Day: " 'See! The Lord has given you the sabbath, therefore on the sixth day he gives you bread for two days; remain every man of you in his place, let no man go out of his place on the seventh day.' So the people rested on the seventh day." To be sure, remaining in one's place does not mean that one may not leave his house, but it does mean that one should remain in his own village, which consists of the settled area of the village as well as its natural environs.

Isaiah alludes to the importance of celebrating the day of rest by "not going your own ways": "If you turn back your foot from the sabbath, from doing your pleasure on my holy day, ... I will make you ride upon the heights of the earth" (Isa 58:13, 14). I stay at home in my village, and with God, I ride upon the heights. When the holy day comes, therefore, it enchants and changes me. I was heavy-laden and now I leave off my burden. With the setting of the sun all is changed; I am changed. I went everywhere; now I stay home; I did everything; now I do one thing: gain refreshment and joy. No wonder, in the Sabbath hymn, we sing,

"Those who keep the Sabbath will rejoice in your kingdom." The Sabbath is when God's kingdom comes. Rightly, then, did Jesus link the two messages: take up my yoke, the son of man is lord of the Sabbath. He could not have made the matter clearer.

When, therefore, I notice the conduct of Jesus' disciples – picking crops on the Sabbath, which is servile labor within creation, rather than the celebration of creation – my curiosity deepens. Jesus' argument appeals to the fact that David's followers took food reserved for the priests. What follows is that if we are hungry, we can do what we have to to get food. But the Sabbath requires preparation in advance, not cooking food on that day; that is the meaning of the statement we noted earlier, prepare each day of the week for the Seventh Day. Not kindling a flame, not carrying objects, not cooking food – these are not silly prohibitions; they form the this-worldly expressions of that act of sanctification that imitates God's act of sanctification of the Seventh Day.

When Jesus further justifies his followers' actions by pointing out that, in the Temple, the priests perform the rites of the cult, so it is all right to do so here, he introduces a very profound argument, making a claim about himself that in its monumental quality parallels what he has said about abandoning father and mother and following him. To understand what he says – and to grasp how surprising I find it – you have to know that the Temple and the world beyond the Temple form mirror images of one another. What we do in the Temple is the opposite of what we do everywhere else.

The Torah is explicit that sacrifices are to be offered on that day. For example, an additional offering for the Sabbath is prescribed in Numbers 28:9–10, 28:3–8; the show bread of the Temple was replaced on the Sabbath Day (Lev 24:8). So it was clear to everybody that what was not to be done outside of the Temple, in secular space, was required to be done in holy space, in the Temple itself. When, therefore, Jesus says that something greater

than the Temple is here, he can only mean that he and his disciples may do on the Sabbath what they do because they stand in
the place of the priests in the Temple: the holy place has shifted,
now being formed by the circle made up of the master and his
disciples.

What troubles me, therefore, is not that the disciples do not
obey one of the rules of the Sabbath. That is trivial and beside the
point. What captures my attention is Jesus' statement that at
stake in their actions is not the Sabbath but the Temple, a truly
fresh formulation of matters. His claim, then, concerns not
whether or not the Sabbath is to be sanctified, but where and
what is the Temple, the place where things are done on the Sabbath that elsewhere are not to be done at all. Not only so, but just
as on the Sabbath it is permitted to place on the altar the food that
is offered up to God, so Jesus' disciples are permitted to prepare
their food on the Sabbath, again a stunning shift indeed.

So why should anyone not have concurred that the intent of
these several statements in sequence – "Come to me, all who labor and are heavy-laden, and I will give you rest"; "you will find
rest for your souls; for my yoke is easy and my burden is light";
"it is lawful to do good on the Sabbath" – is wholly captured in
the simple and necessary conclusion: "For the son of man is lord
of the Sabbath." That, and that alone, is what is at stake in the
master's teachings concerning the one of the Ten Commandments that concerns the Sabbath Day.

Am I to violate two of the Ten Commandments, honoring father and mother, keeping the Sabbath? Scripture itself has linked
the two, as we have already noticed:

> "'You shall fear every man his mother and his father and you shall
> keep my sabbaths' (Lev 19:3).
> "And as a reward? 'If you turn away your foot because of the
> Sabbath, then you shall delight yourself in the Lord' (Isa 58:13–14)."
> (Mekhilta Attributed to Rabbi Ishmael Bahodesh 8 [Neusner: 54:3–5])

Once more, on the surface, what is at stake is Jesus' teaching us to violate two of the Ten Commandments, both of them concerned with the holy life of eternal Israel.

Why doubt Jesus knew the same verses of Scripture that the cited passages introduce? And why wonder whether or not Jesus realized that, in these teachings of his about the Sabbath, he surely appeared not to fulfill but to abolish the Sabbath? Of course he knew perfectly well what the Sabbath meant in the Torah's presentation of it, and obviously he realized how surprising was his decision on the proper conduct of his disciples on the Sabbath. So, it seems to me self-evident, what we face is an irreconcilable conflict. Either "Remember the Sabbath Day to keep it holy" or "The son of man is the Lord of the Sabbath" – but not both.

Once we put the issue in these simple terms, then the solution is obvious. Jesus does not propose to abolish but to fulfill the Torah, and also, Jesus is lord of the Sabbath. Then in keeping the Sabbath in the way in which Jesus represents it, we fulfill the Torah – in the way in which Jesus means it to be fulfilled. And since his way so radically differs from my way, it is clear that we are hearing different voices from Sinai – he for his part, I for mine. Any other conclusion treats as trivial what is a stunning confrontation; the Christ of Faith is speaking here.

Turning back once more to the first of the two addresses on the Sabbath, the one that speaks of rest and refreshment, we recall that coming to God is what is at stake in the Sabbath and its rest: "All things have been delivered to me by my Father, and no one knows the Son except the Father, and no one knows the Father except the Son, and any one to whom the Son chooses to reveal him." These words, by themselves, bear no clear connection to the Sabbath. But these words do *not* stand by themselves. They lead directly into the appeal to come to the father through the son, and then: "Come to me, all who labor and are heavy-laden, and I will give you rest. Take my yoke upon you, and learn from me; for I am gentle and lowly in heart, and you will find rest for your souls. For my yoke is easy and my burden is light."

Sinai's message for the Sabbath scarcely echoes over the distant horizon. And yet if on the Sabbath I do what God did on the first Sabbath, then in very different terms to be sure, Jesus says to his disciples what Moses has said to all Israel. On the Sabbath Day I remember and do what God did: "Remember the sabbath day ... for in six days the Lord made heaven and earth ... and rested on the seventh day; therefore the Lord blessed the sabbath day and hallowed it." Those who seek rest, in Jesus' radical revision, seek God as we seek God; but instead of leaving off their burdens, they take on a new burden: a yoke that is easy and light.

No wonder, then, that the son of man is lord of the Sabbath! The reason is not that he interprets the Sabbath restrictions in a liberal manner, nor yet that he gives good arguments (or not-so-good arguments) for allowing people to harvest and eat their crops that day, or heal the sick and otherwise do good on that day. Jesus was not just another reforming rabbi, out to make life "easier" for people. And no one who keeps the Sabbath so as to imitate God pays much mind to considerations of "lenient" or "strict," except so far as we want to know what God through the Torah wants of us. No, the issue is not that the burden is light. The issue is another one altogether.

Jesus' claim to authority is at issue, not the more lenient, or less lenient, character of his rulings on what we do on the holy day. These counsels simply express in a concrete way a much deeper conviction, and if, as for the purpose of this argument we must concede, he really said these things, then through them he meant to declare himself and his disciples to form a new entity in place of the old.

Nor do these decisions of his – legal rulings, in the context that the Torah would form in time to come – derive from the close reading of scriptural verses that we call exegesis, though they are sustained by exegesis – the close reading – of stories, appeals to accepted facts and arguments as well. The story of David, the fact that the priests do work in the Temple on the Sabbath, the appeal to the obvious rightness of doing good on the Sabbath – all of these really form mere consequences of a fundamental shift that has taken place in his person and presence.

At issue in the Sabbath is neither keeping nor breaking this one of the Ten Commandments. At issue here as everywhere else is the person of Jesus himself, in Christian language, Jesus Christ. What matters most of all is the simple statement that no one knows the Father except the Son and anyone to whom the Son chooses to reveal him. There, startling and scarcely a consequence of anything said before or afterward, stands the centerpiece of the Sabbath-teaching: my yoke is easy, I give you rest, the son of man is lord of the Sabbath indeed, because the son of man is now Israel's Sabbath: how we act like God.

In the very context of the Sabbath, when in sacred space and holy time, Israel acts like God, we grasp that Jesus addresses that very issue – what does it mean to know God – and does so in precisely the context in which Israel, from Sinai, knows God and acts like God: the Sabbath. Jesus has chosen with great precision the message he wishes to set forth with regard to the Sabbath, both the main point, which comes first, and then the details and consequences of that same point, which follow.

When it came to the three of the Ten Commandments that Jesus so richly augmented, I wanted to ask about those other dimensions of my existence – community, family and home, individual and private – that seemed to me neglected. What about the life of Israel in community? In time and in space, Israel in community becomes holy on the enchanted Sabbath Day. Then curtains fall about the village; then families come together in the home; then families form the community at worship and in Torah-study, in the synagogue.

Israel is Israel on the Sabbath: holy, each person doing what God did, all Israel living out the setting of the perfect creation that was blessed and hallowed on that day. I wondered then, where is Jesus' message for me not as a private person, concerned not to kill, commit adultery, take a false oath, but for me as a member of a family, on the one side, and as part of a community, sharing in the social order of the holy people, on the other?

So has Jesus taught me to violate one of the two great commandments among the Ten Commandments, the ones that concern the social order? Of course he has; obviously he has not – it depends on your perspective. From the perspective of the Torah as I understand it, only God is lord of the Sabbath. All things that God wants me to know God has delivered to me in the Torah. All of us know God through the Torah, and it is to all Israel that Moses has revealed the Torah. The Torah teaches me to rest on the Sabbath, because that is how I learn to act like God. All of this Jesus teaches in a different way and for another purpose. He, too, has heard the message of Sinai, but when it comes to the Sabbath, he has taken personally what the rest of Israel have taken to speak to all of us, equally and all at once.

The disciple I meet along the way may argue that that is indeed so: through him we know the Father; through the Sabbath done his way we bear that yoke that is easy, that light burden that is his. Once more, then, the disciple and I concur: Christ now stands on the mountain, he now takes the place of the Torah. That is why he is lord of the Sabbath for those who can affirm that through this son they know the father, uniquely through this son, *the* son. Once more we find ourselves at an impasse – long past disagreement, but not close to a coherent argument at all.

Where then is the argument? What is God's stake in remembering the Sabbath Day? The Torah teaches me that it is my celebrating creation, acting on the Sabbath Day as God acts on the day when creation ceases: blessing the Sabbath Day and sanctifying it. Jesus, too, teaches that the Sabbath Day brings the gift of rest – but it is the rest that God gives through the son. So we find ourselves precisely where we were when we wondered what is at stake in honor of father and mother: keeping the Sabbath forms a this-worldly act of imitation of God. The lord of the Sabbath forms a this-worldly model, in the language of the Torah: "for in six days the Lord made heaven and earth ... therefore the Lord blessed ..." and therefore: "Remember the sabbath day, to keep it holy," by not working, as God stopped working.

So I say to the disciple, is it really so that your master, the son of man, is lord of the Sabbath? Then – so I asked before, so I ask again – is your master God? And that forms the crux of the matter. Is no argument then possible? To the contrary, we may indeed take up a serious argument, the one about perfection. What must I do to be like God? All else has prepared me to address that issue – and to form an argument with not the disciple but the master himself.

Master, if you are lord of the Sabbath, and if by keeping the Sabbath I act like God, then what else must I do to be like God? I know what the Torah teaches me, let me hear your lesson too.

6

You Shall Be Holy;
for I the Lord Your God Am Holy

vs

If You Would Be Perfect, Go,
Sell All You Have and Come,
Follow Me

And behold, one came up to him saying, "Teacher, what good deed must I do to have eternal life?"

And he said to him, "Why do you ask me about what is good? One there is who is good. If you would enter life, keep the commandments."

He said to him, "Which?"

And Jesus said, "You shall not kill. You shall not commit adultery. You shall not steal. You shall not bear false witness. Honor your father and mother (Exod 20:12–16), and, You shall love your neighbor as yourself (Lev 19:18)."

The young man said to him, "All these I have observed, what do I still lack?"

Jesus said to him, "If you would be perfect, go, sell all you have and give to the poor, and you will have treasure in heaven; and come, follow me."

When the young man heard this he went away sorrowful; for he had great possessions."

Matthew 19:16–22

Details of the Ten Commandments, honoring parents or fol- lowing Christ, observing the Sabbath as holy or acknowl- edging the son of man as lord of the Sabbath – these really are the sideshow. All of them are important, but they merely il- lustrate the fundamental issue that Jesus comes to address. But what about the main event – what really counts: What does God want of me? And how can I make myself into what God wants me to be, made me to be? Is there an argument to be constructed about that most fundamental issue? And if I were there, what should I have heard, and how might I have responded to the heart of Jesus' teaching?

Well, imagine that one day I was nearby when I witnessed this wonderful exchange: What must I do to have eternal life? I would have come close to the master to hear his every word: Here is the center of matters, what will happen to me when I die, which is another way of asking, what does God really want me to do and to be in this life?

Jesus, among all us Jews, would take for granted that the Torah answers that question, and all of us together would have under- stood that what I do in this life helps decide what happens to me in eternity. The young man's question is a mature and proper one, and what he really wants the master to tell us all is that when all is said and done, what really counts?

That question, standard and urgent for those Israelites who be- lieve in life after death and the world to come, takes for granted that what I do matters to God, and that God will reward or will punish me for what I do in this life. The young man who asked the question, Jesus and his disciples, and all of us together share this faith. Not only is it a natural question for all of us – What do I have to do to merit eternal life? – but the answer Jesus gives too is true to the Torah: Keep the Ten Commandments and the Great Commandment (Lev 19:18).

Here we have a response wholly in accord with the teaching of the Torah. Had the story ended here, I would have gladly tagged along to hear more from this authentic master of the Torah. For a great master is not one who says what is new, but one who says what is true, and the master I seek is one who speaks to me, who wants to be found by me – so that I, too, may learn what God through the Torah has asked of me.

But the conversation didn't stop. The young man found the answer wanting. As I watched his face, I could see the disappointment. He wanted more than a standard answer. He and I could well have argued about that, for, I would have told him that what the Torah gives is all you get, and all you should want. But he was talking with Jesus, not with me.

The young man: "Is that all? What do I lack?"

Jesus: "Well, if it's perfection you have in mind ..."

The rapid exchange startled me. Jesus shifts the discussion from "what do I have to do to have eternal life" to "if you would be perfect." Here is a profound turn. Jesus has grasped the question the young man really wanted to ask, which was not merely about eternal life but about "perfection" – something else altogether.

This young man wants to be more than mortal, for who aspires to be perfect, accepting what we human beings are? All of us, after all, know the story of Adam and Eve. We remember the sad tale of the Ten Generations from Adam and Eve to Abraham, the descent of humanity to the Flood. Perfection indeed! Let me at least do what God, understanding my frailty, asks: at least (some of) the Ten Commandments, at least "love your neighbor as yourself."

Perfection? Who ever mentioned it, who thought of it? (Mere) eternal life is for mortals, and God understands what and who we are: "The Lord saw that the wickedness of man was great in the earth, and that every imagination of the thoughts of his heart was only evil continually. And the Lord was sorry that he had made man on the earth, and it grieved him in his heart" (Gen 6:5–6). Given the frailty of humanity, none can expect perfection as the price for eternal life.

To understand what is at stake in this exchange, we do well to turn the clock forward for a couple of hundred years and listen to what other masters of the Torah besides Jesus found in response to the issue of what I have to do to gain eternal life or the world to come or life after death or the kingdom of heaven: a mixture of different ways of speaking of the same matter, so it seems to me. They defined matters in a much less restrictive way than did Matthew's Jesus, asking not even for perfect obedience to the Ten Commandments or the Golden Rule of Leviticus 19:18. All they asked for was faith and loyalty to God; a merciful and forgiving God will do the rest.

Indeed, these masters' yoke was easy, their burden light, when they stated very simply: Everybody who believes in life after death will merit life after death, with exceptions of a rare sort:

> All Israelites have a share in the world to come, as it is said, "your people also shall be all righteous, they shall inherit the land forever; the branch of my planting, the work of my hands, that I may be glorified" (Isa 60:21).
>
> And these are the ones who have no portion in the world to come:
>
> He who says, the resurrection of the dead is a teaching which does not derive from the Torah, and the Torah does not come from Heaven; and an Epicurean.
>
> Rabbi Aqiba says, "Also: He who reads in heretical books, and he who whispers over a wound and says, 'I will put none of the diseases upon you which I have put on the Egyptians, for I am the Lord who heals you' (Exod 15:26)."
>
> Abba Saul says, "Also: He who pronounces the divine Name as it is spelled out." (Mishnah-tractate Sanhedrin 11:1)

The contrast between the encompassing definition before us – everybody except a few very rank sinners, heretics mainly, as against only those who keep the principal commandments, on the one side, or still fewer, only the perfect – is stunning. Reading the same Torah as Jesus read, these sages, for reasons we shall see very soon, simply said all the saints – that is, holy people – are saved, and all Israel is holy. So their very doctrine of who, and what, is eternal Israel also instructed them on who shares the world to come, and the Torah defined Israel very simply: "You shall be holy, for I the Lord your God am holy."

But these thoughts of mine have distracted my attention from the conversation between Jesus and his young interlocutor. Not only so, but I would like to ask the master, "Sir, so few?"

But that is not what I really want to ask, and emboldened by the patience of the teacher, I press forward, stand near to hand, and speak up. I rely on his patience, and remembering God's patience with Abraham at Sodom and even Israel through time, trust Jesus that, in asking what I think is a tough question, I shan't be disappointed by an impatient reply.

"Sir, you seem to me to have answered a question the young man didn't ask, and maybe he asked a question you didn't answer. What he wanted to know is what good deed he had to do. He didn't aspire to perfection.

"But in telling him how to be perfect, you have disrupted the very life you promise: 'If you would enter life, keep the commandments.' But if he listens to you, what will become of him? He gives up home and family, cuts his ties to everything and everyone but you: get rid of everything and follow me."

So we find ourselves back among the details: Honor parents or serve the master? Remember the Sabbath or acknowledge the master? Is this really a fair framing of the question?

Again moving the clock forward, I can define matters in a way the master will approve: The choice of wealth as against the Torah is a choice, so why not the choice of wealth as against Christ? So the master, perspicacious and knowing, points me toward a passage in which other sages of this same Torah of Moses at Sinai in time to come would give the same advice – sort of. Jesus in his wisdom looks toward Aqiba, coming along a few decades hence. In time to come, he tells me, there will be a master of the Torah who will tell his disciple to sell all he has – in order to study the Torah.

So, he might fairly claim, "My advice is not so very different from that of the master that is coming along in time ahead":

> Rabbi Tarfon gave to Rabbi Aqiba six silver centenarii, saying to him, "Go, buy us a piece of land, so we can get a living from it and labor in the study of Torah together."
>
> He took the money and handed it over to scribes, Mishnah-teachers, and those who study Torah.
>
> After some time Rabbi Tarfon met him and said to him, "Did you buy the land that I mentioned to you?"
>
> He said to him, "Yes."
>
> He said to him, "Is it any good?"
>
> He said to him, "Yes."
>
> He said to him, "And do you not want to show it to me?"
>
> He took him and showed him the scribes, Mishnah teachers, and people who were studying Torah, and the Torah that they had acquired.
>
> He said to him, "Is there anyone who works for nothing? Where is the deed covering the field?"
>
> He said to him, "It is with King David, concerning whom it is written, 'He has scattered, he has given to the poor, his righteousness endures forever' (Ps 112:9)." (Leviticus Rabbah XXIV:XVI)

What has Aqiba done, if not the same thing that Jesus demanded in a different context: Get rid of worldly possessions, devote all things of value to the Torah. The advice is the same, only the context shifts. We have dwelt long enough on Jesus' teachings to find familiar the counterpart: Sell all you have, give the money away to the poor, and follow me. The equation is the same, but Christ replaces Torah.

And yet, my sense is that matters have come to a radical reduction, moving as we do from perfection to "follow me." Is that the whole message of the master? Of course not, far from it. Once

94

more conversation – it really isn't an argument anymore – shifts from the detail to the main point. But the afternoon is fading, and we have to part.

Later on, a few days having passed, I had the good fortune to hear Jesus taking up this same question, now in straight and simple terms: What in fact does the Torah want from me? No longer an issue of what do I have to do to get what I want, it is framed in a more sincere and innocent, holy way: Just what does God want of me? And Jesus here responded and taught a message of the Torah, telling people what Israel's sages found in the Torah, what the Torah required them to say:

> "Teacher, which is the great commandment in the law?"
>
> And he said to him, "You shall love the Lord your God with all your heart, and with all your soul, and with all your mind. This is the great and first commandment. And a second is like it, You shall love your neighbor as yourself. On these two commandments depend the whole Torah and the prophets." (Matt 22:36–40)

Here we have what is familiar and authentic: to love God, as the *Shema*, the prayer proclaiming God's unity and Israel's submission to God's rule, demands; and to love your neighbor as yourself. No sage could take exception to these teachings. But in how they are elaborated, there is room for argument and exception.

To understand why, we have first of all to examine the context in which the second of the two commandments is set:

> And the Lord said to Moses, "Say to all the congregation of the people of Israel, 'You shall be holy; for I the Lord your God am holy ...'" (Lev 19:1–2)
>
> "You shall not hate your brother in your heart, but you shall reason with your neighbor, lest you bear sin because of him. You shall not take vengeance or bear any grudge against the sons of your own people, but you shall love your neighbor as yourself: I am the Lord." (Lev 19:17–18)

95

If I had to point to one of those "great commandments" of the Torah, I would have said: "Master, there is a third that is like it: 'You shall be holy; for I the Lord your God am holy.'" Here, after all, is a commandment that addresses not me personally and how I love God, or not me in relationship to someone else, but to all of us, all Israel together. Once more, therefore, I am struck by the dimensions of the world that Jesus addresses: the individual in search of salvation, the private person in quest of God. And all due honor for the Torah-teachings that he cites, but the Torah says something about a dimension of human existence that, in these sayings, Jesus does not discern: the community as a whole, all of us together, what in today's language we should call the social order.

Why no message about that third dimension of human existence, besides the life of the human being in relationship to himself or herself, besides the life of one person to another? What about our relationship to God?

Is love of God all there is? Is there no relationship of us all before God? I can love God and my neighbor and yet live in Sodom. But God destroyed Sodom. So God surely cares about more than humanity, one by one by one. God cares about humanity, all at once and all together. And that is – so the Torah teaches – the reason that God called Abraham and Sarah, Isaac and Rebecca, Jacob and Leah and Rachel – and loved their children enough to give them the Torah at Sinai.

That is why, in my mind, what Jesus has not said takes on profound weight; he has spoken to me, but not to us; there is no dimension of holy and eternal Israel in his reading of the Torah's fundamental teaching. He has said that I should sell all I have, give to the poor, and follow him; Aqiba in context told Tarfon no less. But he has not said that we – not I, but we, Israel – are to be; how are we, eternal Israel, to strive to be like God. After all, "loving your neighbor as yourself" (Lev 19:18) comes at the end of the very passage that commences with, "You shall be holy; for I ... am holy." Since Jesus knows the Torah at least as well as anybody else, he has made his choices, selecting what counts and silently bypassing what does not. That, after all, is to be expected from a master so original in his teachings about the fence around the Torah: "You have heard it said ... but I say to you ..." Here the thought passes my mind, he might have said, "You have heard it said ... but I don't say that to you ..."

So in bypassing the foundation statement at Leviticus 19:2–3, of which the concluding statement comes as a climax at Leviticus 19:18, Jesus has – so it seems to me – left the main point out of his message. Why should I love my neighbor as myself? Because – so Moses has taught us – "you shall be holy, for I the Lord your God am holy." And that is part of what it means to be like God, to strive for holiness like God's. All the rest of that chapter of the Torah, reaching its climax with the second of the two great commandments, forms a commentary on the commandment of holiness; and that commandment Jesus has not mentioned.

In all fairness to the master, I owe him my criticism. What kind of respect would I show if I just dismissed him in my mind and gave him no chance to respond?

"Sir," I ask, "how about 'You shall be holy'? What does the Torah want me to be when it tells me to be holy?"

He motions me to continue.

"In fact, my lord, our sages of blessed memory find in the commandment to be holy all of the Ten Commandments, and to be holy means to keep those commandments. So our sages teach." And again relying upon the perspicacity of a master to foresee the lessons later sages would derive from the Torah he knew so well, I would have pointed into the future for the exposition.

"May I go on?"

A nod.

"Sir," I say to him, "in time to come, sages will read the Torah and show how this very passage that we study together – Leviticus 19, which teaches Israel to be holy – goes over the Ten Commandments. They will demonstrate, and I'll show you how, that

97

in the commandments of Leviticus 19 are the Ten Commandments of Exodus 20. So there is a good reason for me to keep the
Ten Commandments, and that is, so that I shall be holy, because
God is holy. I want to be like God, and the Ten Commandments,
restated in Leviticus 19, teach me how to be like God.

"Sir, will you have the patience to hear out the way in which, in
a time to come, a rabbi will spell all this out for us?" He nods, and
I proceed:

Rabbi Hiyya taught, "[The statement, 'Say to all the congregation of
the people of Israel' (Lev 19:2)] teaches that the entire passage was
stated on the occasion of the gathering [of the entire assembly].

"And what is the reason that it was stated on the occasion of the gathering [of the entire assembly]? Because the majority of the principles of
the Torah depend upon [what is stated in this chapter of the Torah]."

Rabbi Levi said, "It is because the Ten Commandments are encom-
passed within its [teachings].

"'I am the Lord your God' (Exod 20:2), and here it is written, 'I am the
Lord your God' (Lev 19:2).

"'You shall have no [other gods]' (Exod 20:3), and here it is written,
'You shall not make for yourselves molten gods' (Lev 19:4).

"'You shall not take [the name of the Lord your God in vain]' (Exod
20:7), and here it is written, 'You shall not take a lying oath by my
name' (Lev 19:12).

"'Remember the Sabbath day' (Exod 20:8), and here it is written, 'You
will keep my Sabbaths' (Lev 19:3).

"'Honor your father and your mother' (Exod 20:12), and here it is
written, 'Each person shall fear his mother and his father' (Lev 19:3).

"'You shall not murder' (Exod 20:13), and here it is written, 'You shall
not stand idly by the blood of your neighbor' (Lev 19:16).

"'You shall not commit adultery' (Exod 20:13), and here it is written,
'Do not profane your daughter by making her a harlot' (Lev 19:29).

"'You shall not steal' (Exod 20:13), and here it is written, 'You shall
not steal and you shall not deal falsely' (Lev 19:11).

" 'You shall not bear false witness [against your neighbor]' (Exod 20:13), and here it is written, 'You shall not go about as a talebearer among your people' (Lev. 19:16).

"You shall not covet' (Exod 20:14), and here it is written, 'And you shall love your neighbor as yourself' " (Lev 19:18). (Leviticus Rabbah 24:5)

There is a moment of silence. The conversation pauses. The young man, the master, and I reflect for a moment on what has passed among us. "You shall be holy ... love your neighbor as yourself ..." – these form nothing more than a recapitulation of the Ten Commandments! How then can someone say, "I've done it all, what more is there?"

Then I speak up again: "When the young man asked what he had to do to 'enter the life of the world to come,' you told him to keep the commandments. Well and good. And when I heard what you said, I thought of why I am taught by the Torah to keep those commandments, and that is, because I want to be holy, because God is holy."

A voice in the crowd: "Holier than thou?"

"No – just holy, because God is holy."

I go on: "Now when God speaking through Moses tells me how to keep the Ten Commandments, he says it is so that I may be holy like God. Isn't that enough?"

The crowd comes closer. "Who said it wasn't enough?"

I remind him, "The young man asked that very question: 'All these I have observed, what do I still lack?' And you answered him quite clearly. He still lacks something. 'If you would be perfect, go, sell all you have and give to the poor, and you will have treasure in heaven, and come, follow me.' So there we have it again, sir.

"What I hear you saying is, the Ten Commandments are not enough, the Great Commandment, the Golden Rule – these, too, are not enough. Perfection consists in poverty and obedience to Christ."

Well, precisely what do I offer as a counter? Jesus contrasts Christ and wealth, as Aqiba later on would contrast Torah and wealth. I have no argument with him on that score. But a more troubling issue persists. Jesus wants me to follow him and be like him. Have I heard such a commandment in the Torah? Of course I have: "You shall be holy; for I the Lord your God am holy." I am called upon by the Torah to try to be like God: holy. (I'll have more to say about that in my argument with Jesus about the Pharisees, which is coming in the next chapter.) But we have come a long way and reached our goal: the possibility of an argument about the main point.

For here we stand at the center of matters. And at this point we find grounds for an argument in which both parties talk about the same things and in the same terms, as I have already shown. Sell all I have and –

– study the Torah
– follow Christ
– Which?

Surely we can now argue about the same matter in the same terms, namely, what is the truly highest value in life? For what should I give my life? That is what is at stake; and well does Jesus answer by saying, "follow me"; and well does the Torah answer by saying, "be holy, for I am holy."

For what difference does it make to the Christian or the Jew if, in either case, we hold "all that we have" to be worth what we most value, which is Christ or the Torah, respectively? No difference at all: the structure is the same. The argument can commence. About what? About the main chance: What is life about? What makes life worth living? Christ and the Torah concur that God answers that question. Christ and the Torah agree that to be perfect, I must strive to be holy like God, or I must give up everything for Christ.

So which? What, then, does the Torah teach me that I am supposed to do in order to imitate God, to be like God? And what, then, does Jesus teach me that I am supposed to do in order to follow Christ? And how are we to choose between these two matched counterparts: two answers to one question, two readings of one Torah?

Here I cannot argue with Jesus. For an honest and fair answer in behalf of Matthew's Jesus would require us to move far beyond the limits of our argument. I said we should argue only with Jesus' teachings, not calling into doubt any detail of Matthew's "good news" about what Jesus did, the miracles he wrought, the messages he gave to his disciples, what was done to him, and how he triumphed over death.

But to accomplish an argument between Christ and Torah, the entire picture of Christ (in Christian language) demands its place at centerstage, and not Matthew's Christ alone, but Mark's and Luke's and John's, and Paul's – and above all, the Christ of the Church and the faithful Christians from then to now. That testimony about what it means to sell all you have and follow me cannot be reduced to a few simple propositions about love for neighbor.

We should, indeed, have to retell the entire Gospel of Matthew in order to answer the question: How shall I try to follow Christ? What does it mean to do so? For not in the teachings of Jesus alone, with which we concern ourselves, is the answer to that question to be found, but in everything he did, and in his submission to God's will in everything that was done to him; and not only so, but also, and especially, in his days in hell and rise from the grave: everything all together, all at once. It would be presumptuous on my part to propose to answer only on the basis of the handful of sayings I find susceptible to argument the question: What must I do when I come to follow him?

And the same is so for the Torah. To set into juxtaposition – and conflict – the account that the Torah provides of what it means to strive to be holy, like God, I should hardly do justice to the matter by merely quoting a few verses of the Torah. I should have to call on all the masters of the Torah from then to now, all those who have studied the Torah with learning and wisdom and, each one in order, set forth for here and now what it means to be holy, like God. For we have come to the heart of matters, and the conflict is a very real one.

Limiting ourselves to Matthew's representation of Jesus, on the one side, and the Torah, on the other,* we find ourselves unworthy of the task. And that is how it should be. For who in the end has the perspective upon things to compare and contrast Christ and the Torah, eternal Israel and the Church – who but God? And God is not party to this argument, except that it concerns the Torah God gave to eternal Israel, on the one side, and the Torah Christ made over, in his time and in his way and through his Church, to Christianity, on the other side.

But leaving the final say to God, perhaps even in the here and now, we may point to the outlines of the argument: Where do we differ, and where do we, eternal Israel, register our dissent?

If we examine what our sages teach we must do in order to be holy, like God, the beginnings of a fair exchange may be discerned. If I had to point to the single difference between the message of the Torah, at least as our sages mediate that message, and the message of Jesus as Matthew quotes and portrays that mes-

---

* I have made reference, also, to documents that, in Judaism, are regarded as part of the Torah, but are not in the Hebrew Scriptures or "Old Testament." These are the Mishnah, defined earlier, the two Talmuds (the Talmud of the Land of Israel, ca. A.D. 400, and the Talmud of Babylonia, ca. A.D. 600), which form extensions and amplifications of the Mishnah, and various compilations of interpretations of Scripture, called Midrash-compilations, which form extensions and amplifications of the (written part of the) Torah. For the sake of argument, we need not quibble; for Judaism these all are part of the one whole Torah given by God to Moses at Mount Sinai. It is the fact that none of these writings had come to closure by the time of Jesus, but only many centuries later. But in an argument between religions, just as for the purposes of argument I invoke Matthew's Jesus as Christianity has affirmed that gospel of Jesus (among others) so I represent "the Torah" as Judaism defines the Torah. Religions don't argue about historical facts but about God's truth, and that is what I mean to do.

sage, it is in one simple fact: The message of the Torah always concerns eternal Israel. The message of Jesus Christ always concerns those who follow him.

The Torah always speaks to the community and concerns itself with the formation of a social order worthy of God who called Israel into being. Jesus Christ in Matthew's account speaks of everything but the social order of the here and now; here he speaks of himself and his circle; then, in time to come, he speaks of the kingdom of heaven.

Lost in between the man and the coming kingdom is the everyday of the common life. But it is that everyday, common life that the Torah commands Israel to sanctify. And at stake in that life of a social order aimed at sanctification is nothing less than the sanctification of God on high.

So I turn once more to the master, imposing on his patience to be sure, with this insistence of mine: "We matter not only one by one by one, but all together, all at once. Holiness is not for thee and me, but for all of us: we all, all together all at once, are the ones to whom God spoke when, using the plural 'you,' God said, 'You shall be holy; for I the Lord your God am holy.' God uses the plural 'you' nearly always, and in these critical, emblematic sayings of yours" – I speak now to Matthew's Jesus – "the 'you' is – well, a young man. What about all Israel – that 'you' of 'you shall be holy, for I ...'

"Let me spell out, sir, what is at stake, as our sages in time to come would explain matters. When Israel forms a social world that conveys the sanctity of life, then Israel sanctifies God." Then, taking license with time, I point to this statement:

"You shall be holy, for I the Lord your God am holy:"
That is to say, "If you sanctify yourselves, I shall credit it to you as though you had sanctified me, and if you do not sanctify yourselves, I shall hold that it is as if you have not sanctified me."
Or perhaps the sense is this: "If you sanctify me, then lo, I shall be sanctified, and if not, I shall not be sanctified"?

Scripture says, "For I ... am holy," meaning, I remain in my state of sanctification, whether or not you sanctify me.

Abba Saul says, "The king has a retinue, and what is the task thereof? It is to imitate the king." (Sifra CXCV:I.2–3)

To this the disciples of Christ must surely respond, "That indeed is our faith: to imitate Christ." To that we devote our lives. So wherein do we differ, and how come you take exception? Why the great dissent?

My answer comes to me from our sages' exposition of the details of imitating God, of being like God, of being holy like God. In our times the accusation that one is "holier than thou," which no one wants to admit but many would like to be, gives a bad name to sanctification. So we do well to hear what Israel's sages make of this commandment to be like God.

Here is how our sages of blessed memory read some of the critical verses before us:

"You shall not take vengeance [or bear any grudge]:"

To what extent is the force of vengeance?

If one says to him, "Lend me your sickle," and the other did not do so.

On the next day, the other says to him, "Lend me your spade."

The one then replies, "I am not going to lend it to you, because you didn't lend me your sickle."

In that context, it is said, "You shall not take vengeance."

"or bear any grudge:"

To what extent is the force of a grudge?

If one says to him, "Lend me your spade," but he did not do so.

The next day the other one says to him, "Lend me your sickle," and the other replies, "I am not like you, for your didn't lend me your spade [but here, take the sickle]!"

In that context, it is said, "or bear any grudge."

"but you shall love your neighbor as yourself: [I am the Lord]:"

Rabbi Aqiba says, "This is the encompassing principle of the Torah." (Sifra CC:III.4, 5, 7)

Being holy like God means not taking vengeance in any form, even in words; not pointing out to the other that I have not acted in the nasty way he did. In many ways, we find ourselves at home. This counsel recalls, after all, the message that if the Torah says not to murder, then we must not even risk becoming angry. Loving God means going the extra mile. Aqiba has the climax and conclusion "love your neighbor as yourself" as the great commandment, the encompassing principle, of the entire Torah.

And that brings us to the next question. Precisely what then does it mean to be "like God"? Here is one answer:

> Abba Saul says, "O try to be like him:
> "Just as he is gracious and merciful, you too be gracious and merci-ful"[add: for it is said, "The Lord, God, merciful and gracious" (Exod 34:6)]. (Mekhilta Attributed to Rabbi Ishmael XVIII:II.3)

To be like God means to imitate the grace and mercy of God: these are what make God God, and these are what can make us like God. So to be like God is to be very human. But to be human in a very special way: it is, after all, the grace of God that in the end accords to us the strength to be merciful and gracious – the grace, but also the example. Not a few followers of Jesus will point to him in this way, just as we point to God in this way.

And here is another along the same lines. In what follows, a sage asks how we can follow God or be like God; that is, what does it mean to be holy, like God? And the answer is, it means to imitate God, to do the things that God does, as the Torah portrays God's deeds:

> And Rabbi Hama ben Rabbi Hanina said, "What is the meaning of the following verse of Scripture: 'You shall walk after the Lord your God' (Deut 13:5).
> "Now is it possible for a person to walk after the Presence of God? And has it not been said, 'For the Lord your God is a consuming fire' (Deut 4:24)?

"But the meaning is that one must walk after the traits of the Holy One, blessed be he.

"Just as he clothes the naked, as it is written, 'And the Lord God made for Adam and for his wife coats of skin and clothed them' (Gen 3:21), so should you clothe the naked.

"[Just as] the Holy One, blessed be he, visited the sick, as it is written, 'And the Lord appeared to him by the oaks of Mamre' (Gen 18:1), so should you visit the sick.

"[Just as] the Holy One, blessed be he, comforted the mourners, as it is written, 'And it came to pass after the death of Abraham that God blessed Isaac his son' (Gen 25:11), so should you comfort the mourners.

"[Just as] the Holy One, blessed be he, buried the dead, as it is written, 'And he buried him in the valley' (Deut 34:6), so should you bury the dead." (Babylonian Talmud tractate Sotah 14A)

So to be holy like God, I must clothe the naked, visit the sick, comfort the mourner, bury the dead – "love my neighbor as myself." These again are very human traits, loving traits. It is not for nothing that, in the Torah, we are told that we are made in God's image, after God's likeness: "So God created man in his own image, in the image of God he created him; male and female he created them" (Gen 1:27). No wonder, then, that the Torah's sages would find the holiness of God in clothing the naked, visiting the sick, comforting the mourner, burying the dead – maybe even teaching Torah to prisoners.

At this point, Jesus will surely have wanted to say, "Well, what in the world do you think I've been telling you all this time?"

I nod: "Yes. I know. But ..."

Then, with infinite tact and courtesy, he nods and goes on his way; we part friends. No ifs, ands, or buts: just friends.

He has, indeed, said no less; but he has said much more. So while we part friends, he goes his way, the young man who brought us together turns sadly homeward – and I find the nearest synagogue.

For it nears dark, and I have my prayers to recite – and also the responsibility of studying a little of the Torah. Joining the assembled Israel of that town, I turn to recite the prayers for dusk, beginning: "Happy are those who dwell in your house, they will once more praise you. Happy the people to whom such blessings fall! Happy the people whose God is the Lord!" (Ps 144:15).

After we complete the prayer for dusk, we gather around our master in the darkening room. In the Torah-study session that evening, he says, "Tell me what's on your mind? Ask me something, and I'll see if I can answer."

So I ask the master what it's all about: the Torah has so much in it. The master, Jesus, after all, has explained what the important commandments are. He can put it altogether in a few simple words, and much that he says makes sense in line with the teaching of the Torah. Can you tell me what the Torah is all about? Are all the commandments the same, or is one more important than another? And what does it mean, when you come down to it, "to be holy, because God is holy"?

So I lay out what has been on my mind all day long: "Teacher, what good deed must I do to have eternal life?"

The sun has set, darkness covering the village beyond. In the lamplight, the master points out that the Torah itself answers that same question that the master, Jesus, has been asked: What does it all add up to? Indeed, from Moses onward, great prophets – David, Isaiah, Micah, Amos, Habakkuk – told us what counts. And here (as a later master put their teachings together) is what they said:

> Rabbi Simelai expounded, "Six hundred and thirteen commandments were given to Moses, three hundred and sixty-five negative ones, corresponding to the number of the days of the solar year, and two hundred forty-eight positive commandments, corresponding to the parts of man's body."

"David came and reduced them to eleven: 'A Psalm of David: Lord, who shall sojourn in thy tabernacle, and who shall dwell in thy holy mountain? (i) He who walks uprightly and (ii) works righteousness and (iii) speaks truth in his heart and (iv) has no slander on his tongue and (v) does no evil to his fellow and (vi) does not take up a reproach against his neighbor, (vii) in whose eyes a vile person is despised but (viii) honors those who fear the Lord. (ix) He swears to his own hurt and changes not. (x) He does not lend on interest. (xi) He does not take a bribe against the innocent' (Ps 15).

"Isaiah came and reduced them to six: '(i) He who walks righteously and (ii) speaks uprightly, (iii) he who despises the gain of oppressions, (iv) shakes his hand from holding bribes, (v) stops his ear from hearing of blood (vi) and shuts his eyes from looking upon evil, he shall dwell on high' (Isa 33:25–26).

"Micah came and reduced them to three: 'It has been told you, man, what is good, and what the Lord demands from you, (i) only to do justly and (ii) to love mercy, and (iii) to walk humbly before God' (Mic 6:8).

"Isaiah again came and reduced them to two: 'Thus says the Lord, (i) Keep justice and (ii) do righteousness' (Isa 56:1).

"Amos came and reduced them to a single one, as it is said, 'For thus says the Lord to the house of Israel. Seek Me and live.'

"Habakkuk further came and based them on one, as it is said, 'But the righteous shall live by his faith' (Hab 2:4)." (Babylonian Talmud Makkot 24A-B)

"So," the master says, "is this what the sage, Jesus, had to say?"
I: "Not exactly, but close."
He: "What did he leave out?"
I: "Nothing."
He: "Then what did he add?"
I: "Himself."
He: "Oh."
I: " 'But the righteous shall live by his faith.' And what is that? 'It has been told you, man, what is good, and what the Lord

demands from you, only to do justly and to love mercy, and to walk humbly before God.'"

He: "Would Jesus agree?"

I: "I think so."

He: "Well, why so troubled this evening?"

I: "Because I really believe there is a difference between 'You shall be holy, for I the Lord your God am holy and 'If you would be perfect, go, sell all you have and come, follow me.'"

He: "I guess then it really depends on who the 'me' is."

I: "Yes, it depends."

He: "And now it's time for the evening prayer: you lead us."

I open with the lines with which the evening prayer commences, which speak of how God loves us: "'And he, being merciful, forgives iniquity and does not destroy, abundantly turns his anger away and does not engage all his wrath: O Lord, save us, King, answer us when we call.

I proceed to the call to prayer: "'Bless the Lord who is to be blessed ...'"

With all my heart and with all my soul, I recite the Shema: "'Hear, Israel, the Lord our God is the one God. And you shall love the Lord your God with all your heart, with all your soul, and with all your might.'"

So then, as always, we offered our evening prayers to the living God. And in some village across the valley, so did Jesus, and his disciples, and all of eternal Israel, the holy people, living in the holy land, greeting nightfall. They did that then, and we, eternal Israel, do that even now, bowing our knee as we speak to the blessed one, God of Abraham and Sarah, Isaac and Rebecca, Jacob and Leah and Rachel, all of us: the Abrahams and Isaacs and Jacobs and Sarahs and Rebeccas and Leahs and Rachels who were then and are now eternal Israel.

It is now dark. The sun has set, the stars come out. Our prayers end. And we end now as we did then, with words that Jesus used too:

Let the holy name of God be sanctified and made great in the world that God created in accord with God's will. And may God's kingdom come to rule, in your lifetime, and in the lifetime of all Israel, and say, Amen.

Our father who is in heaven, may your name be sanctified. Your will be done, your kingdom come, on earth as it is in heaven ...

So we prayed that night, so we pray through time; so he prayed that night, so his disciples would pray through time. Yes, we argue and contend: but we pray to the same God. And that in the end is why we shall always contend and argue, but serve God by loving one another, as God loves us.

But how does God show that love for us?

The next morning was a Thursday, when the holy Torah is removed from the ark and displayed to eternal Israel and read aloud. Being of the priesthood, I am called to the Torah first. And I say the blessing that we say before reading the words of the Torah:

Blessed are you, Lord, our God, ruler of the world, who has chosen us from among all peoples and give us the Torah. Blessed are you ... who gives the Torah.

Gives – here, now, every day.

And afterward:

Blessed are you, Lord, our God, ruler of the world, who has given us a true Torah, and so planted in us life forever. Blessed are you ... who gives the Torah.

That is how God shows that love for us. I left the synagogue services and looked to the far horizon. And I was glad to be who I was, and where I was, and what I was – along with all Israel then and now and forever.

7

You Shall Be Holy
vs
Holier Than Thou

Then said Jesus to the crowds and to his disciples, "The scribes and the Pharisees sit on Moses' seat; so practice and observe whatever they tell you, but not what they do; for they preach, but do not practice. They bind heavy burdens, hard to bear, and lay them on men's shoulders; but they themselves do not move them with their finger. They do all their deeds to be seen by men; for they make their phylacteries broad and their fringes long, and they love the place of honor at feasts and the best seats in the synagogues, and salutations in the market places, and being called rabbi by men. But you are not to be called rabbi, for you have one teacher, and you are all brethren.

Matthew 23:1–8

Clearly, it is one thing to be holy; it is another to be holier than thou. And easy and gentle though his yoke may be, the master, Jesus, has some pretty harsh things to say on people who make themselves out to be better than others. And this bothers me – a lot. The reason is not because plenty of Jesus'

111

criticisms of pious people in his time could well be addressed to pious people I know in synagogues today. A religion that teaches, as Judaism does, that God wants us to do certain things and not do other things is going to produce people who make a big deal about the do's and the don'ts, without paying attention to God's purpose in telling us to do or not to do. So a religion that comes to this worldly expression can well find more than its share of people who do it all for show. That does not make that religion worthless; what it does is underline problems natural to that way of serving God. But God knows what's going on, and so do we.

What bothers me in Jesus' harsh judgments about the scribes and Pharisees is that I'm one of those people who do the things that the scribes and Pharisees observe.* That is to say, I really do believe that God wants me to carry out the Torah; I believe that God wants me to strive to be holy. Jesus lays down so vigorous a barrage of criticisms of people like me that, from that time to our own day, Pharisee loses its capital *P*, and a pharisee is a hypocrite: "They do all their deeds to be seen by men." And that judgment about Judaism (not to mention the forms of Christianity, and they are very many, who also do deeds to serve God, and believe God

---

* The scribes practiced a profession and were responsible for teaching the Torah, for preparing the documents that made official actions in conformity with the Torah. For example, a woman was entitled to a marriage contract, which specified the husband's responsibilities to her while she was married and also in the event of a divorce or the death of the husband. The scribes would write such a document. If a woman was divorced, her husband had to give her a writ of divorce. That severed the marriage. Since the marriage was sanctified on high, the proper writing and delivery of a writ of divorce here on earth meant that, in Heaven, the woman was no longer sanctified to that particular man and was now free to marry any other man. So the scribe on earth was a partner of Heaven both in his teaching of the Torah and also in many of the documents that he prepared. The Pharisees were ordinary people who kept certain laws of the Torah in an extraordinary way. Later in this chapter I shall explain in some detail some of their beliefs and practices and place into context the argument that Jesus had with them.

is pleased by those deeds) concerns not only hypocrites or people who do it all for show. It concerns everybody who carries out the religious duties, the *mitzvot* or commandments, that the Torah teaches.

We who try to obey the Torah and do the mitzvot believe that that is how we carry out the covenant that joins us to God: it is what the Torah tells us God wants us to do as our part of the covenanted relationship between us and God. It is a life under the rules of the Torah because these rules form the terms of the covenant. When I keep the commandments of the Torah, I serve God. When I do a commandment, I recite the blessing, "Blessed are you, Lord, our God, ruler of the world, who has sanctified us by the commandments, and commanded us to ...," and then I refer to the deed that I do. This is what the life under the Torah aims for: the sanctification of everyday life, through the doing, for God's sake, of everyday deeds. But back to these harsh judgments, and the argument that I have to present to the master in response to them.

But I would not for one minute suggest that Jesus was not provoked to anger. Time and again opponents of his – out-and-out enemies – turned out to be Pharisees, sometimes along with Sadducees,† sometimes along with scribes. And Jesus had enemies, and had solid reason to be provoked by them. We have no reason to gloss over the strong hostility among these different groups of Jewish believers. For example, when they came to be baptized by John the Baptist – that is, washed in water, in Matthew's meaning, to be cleansed from sin – John the Baptist rejected them: "You brood of vipers! Who warned you to flee from

---

† The Sadducees are represented also as a group with special beliefs and viewpoints, both in religious and in political life. They differed from the Pharisees in that, while the Pharisees believed in life after death and the world to come, the Sadducees did not.

the wrath to come?" Jesus himself was constantly asked questions – and not very friendly ones at that – by these same people.

The Pharisees asked his disciples, "Why does your teacher eat with tax collectors and sinners?" (Matt 9:11). The disciples of John the Baptist asked, "Why do we and the Pharisees fast, but your disciples do not fast" (Matt 9:14). When he did wonders, "the Pharisees said, 'He casts out demons by the prince of demons'" (Matt 9:34, so too Matt 12:24). Then again, they tried to trip him up: "Look, your disciples are doing what is not lawful to do on the sabbath" (Matt 12:2). When he healed on the Sabbath, "the Pharisees went out and took counsel against him, how to destroy him" (Matt 12:14). And they wanted a sign, "Teacher, we wish to see a sign from you" (Matt 12:38). So Jesus certainly had solid reason to rebuke the Pharisees, among his other opponents and enemies. And he gave as good as he got.

I heard about these provocations and answers but could make very little sense of most of them. Certainly, Jesus said some things that accorded with the Torah. He said some that made the Torah even more compelling. And he said many things that were very much his own. Some of the Pharisees' challenges – How come your folk don't keep the Sabbath? How about some sort of sign or wonder? – derived from the convictions of people in general. But some were very special to them – and Jesus clearly objected, in the strongest possible language, to particular practices and beliefs that he thought distinctive to the Pharisees.

One day I happened along as one of these confrontations got underway. Somebody said something, then someone else joined in, and before we knew it, feelings overflowed. Pharisees on the one side, reddened in the noonday sun, Jesus and his disciples on the other, glared back, heat in their eyes. It all started with a very simple question, the sort of ongoing harassment that Jesus had to put up with from day to day, and I was embarassed by it and sorry that so interesting a figure was not getting the hearing he deserved:

Then Pharisees and scribes came to Jesus from Jerusalem and said, "Why do your disciples transgress the tradition of the elders? For they do not wash their hands when they eat."

He answered them, "And why do you transgress the commandment of God for the sake of your tradition? For God commanded, 'Honor your father and your mother,' and 'He who speaks evil of father or mother, let him surely die.' But you say, 'If any one tells his father or his mother, What you would have gained from me is given to God, he need not honor his father.' So, for the sake of your tradition, you have made void the word of God. You hypocrites! Well did Isaiah prophesy of you when he said:

'This people honors me with their lips, but their heart is far from me; in vain do they worship me, teaching as doctrines the precepts of men' (Isa 29:13)." (Matt 15:1–9)

As I said, the one thing I came to expect from Jesus was a good argument. This matter of "washing hands when they eat," which was presented as "a tradition of the elders," was important to the Pharisees but ridiculous to Jesus. Washing hands was not for hygienic purposes; this conversation took place long before anybody ever heard of microbes.

So this brings us back to the Pharisees and leads us to want to know what they did, or didn't do, that made them special. The rite in question concerned purification. To understand what this meant, we have first of all to put out of our minds any conception that purity or cleanness had any physical aspect. So what is at stake here? A glimpse at the answer comes in an important statement in the Mishnah, later on, which places into relationship a number of things:

Rabbi Pinhas ben Yair says, "Heedfulness leads to cleanliness, cleanliness leads to cleanness, cleanness leads to abstinence, abstinence leads to holiness, holiness leads to modesty, modesty leads to the fear of sin, the fear of sin leads to piety, piety leads to the Holy Spirit, the Holy Spirit leads to the resurrection of the dead, and the resurrection of the dead comes through Elijah, blessed be his memory, Amen." (Mishnah-tractate Sotah 9:14)

In this context, we see how a variety of virtues forms a ladder, upward to heaven. We start with attentiveness or heedfulness, paying close attention to what we do. This is one of the reasons that an excess of attentiveness can lead to those bad traits I mentioned at the outset: too much of a good thing. That then does lead to personal cleanliness, and that proceeds to that "cleanness" that is at stake here. From there, that is, from cleanness (or purification), for a reason I'll spell out in a minute, we get to holiness, and that leads us from these virtues of holiness to the more important virtues of ethics and morality: modesty, fear of sin, piety, and upward to the resurrection of the dead. So the issues are not trivial.

Well, moving from theory to practice, for what reason did I want then to be "holy," and why should I want to be "clean" or "pure"? Now in that time and place, being "holy" meant in part being "holy" for a particular purpose, and one of the distinctive reasons for "holiness" was to go to the Temple and participate in its rites. The priests in particular were described as holy; the food they ate, which they received from the altar or from God's share of the crops of the land, was holy; and they had to observe certain rules in connection with eating it.

These rules are described by Moses in the book of Leviticus in the language of "holiness"; and while, as we realize, "to be holy, for God is holy" means to keep the Ten Commandments, to be holy in that very same context in Leviticus means also to observe certain purity laws. And, all parties clearly agree, one of these rules was to wash hands before eating, so removing whatever minor uncleanness affected them.

When the Pharisees asked Jesus how come his disciples didn't keep this "tradition of the elders," not washing hands before meals, what they wanted to know was, "Why aren't 'you people' interested in holiness, the way we are?" That question represented both a compliment and a challenge. They wanted Jesus to be like them. That was the compliment. But the challenge was, "Why aren't you like us, with us?"

Jesus' answer set up a contrast between this "tradition of the elders" and the commandments of God. He said you place these traditions over the clear statement of God. This they did by observing another law of the Torah, which has to do with vow-taking. Moses had told Israel, "When you take a vow ... you shall not break your word; you shall do according to all that proceeds out of your mouth" (cf. Num. 30: 2). Now one of the things that people would do is declare something holy: that is, to be in the category of an offering on the altar.

What this meant was that no one could use or enjoy the thing that had been declared holy; that would have been an act of sacrilege. Jesus makes a very simple point: By allowing such nonsense to go on, you make it possible for people even to treat their parents disrespectfully. They could declare something "an offering" and so deprive their parents the right to make use of that thing. That is the sense of the language, "What you would have gained from me is given to God."

Listening to this exchange, all I could think was, "But ... but ... but ..." because neither side seemed to me to speak to the issue of the other. It made me think of the first and only argument I had with my wife, when I said I thought supper was mediocre. To which she replied, "Yeah, and your driving stinks." I never again criticized supper, and she never raised the subject of driving again; but supper got better, and I slowed down.

But that's not what happened that day. The Pharisees wanted to know why Jesus didn't care about eating food in a state of sanctification. And he answered, because there is something more important. And his answer chose a good point, because the case he introduced pertained to sanctification. If someone declared something holy ("What you would have gained from me is given to God"), then that person would end up placing considerations of holiness over the requirements of the Ten Commandments – a very solid reply.

But –

But the question and the counterquestion scarcely met, so it seemed to me. All the Pharisees wanted to know is why "you people" – Jesus' disciples – weren't Pharisees; they were welcome and wanted. Living life in accord with the rules of holiness was something Pharisees valued; in their mind was what God wants when he says, "You shall be holy; for I the Lord your God am holy." And in time to come, people would say in so many words precisely what that meant: to live in accord with the rules of the Pharisees.

And what Jesus said in reply was that there are other commandments of the Torah that are more important than this tradition of the fathers. But the way "you people" observe your tradition, you make the law a joke.

So the question went in one direction, the answer in another, and I stood there, very uncomfortable, in the noonday sun, in the heat of an argument that led nowhere. No wonder the harsh words that Jesus addressed to these particular people. What Jesus time and again maintained of "you people" was that they were hypocrites – don't do what they say. And if you do what they say, it will do no good.

So for instance, another time, the Pharisees came to challenge Jesus on the matter of divorce: Is divorce ever legitimate? (cf. Matt 19:3).

Now as a matter of fact, they knew the answer perfectly well, since Deuteronomy 24:1ff. makes provision for divorce: "When a man takes a wife and marries her, if then she finds no favor in his eyes because he has found some indecency in her, and he writes her a bill of divorce and puts it in her hand and sends her out of his house and she departs out of his house, and if she goes and becomes another man's wife, and the latter husband dislikes her and writes her a bill of divorce and puts it in her hand and sends her out of his house, or if the latter husband dies, who took her to be his wife, then her former husband, who sent her away, may not take her again to be his wife ..." (Deut 24:1–4). So God's instruction to Moses took for granted that there can be a divorce.

But Jesus answered the question "Is divorce ever legitimate?" in a different way. He said that "the two shall become one" (Gen 1:27) means "what God has joined together, let no man put asunder."

So the Pharisees fairly wondered how this answered the question since, after all, Moses himself had made provision for a divorce. And that is precisely what the Pharisees pointed out.

Jesus responded with yet another observation that the Torah provides for how people really are. Ideally, there would be no divorce: "For your hardness of heart Moses allowed you to divorce your wives ... and I say to you: whoever divorces his wife, except for unchastity, and marries another, commits adultery" (Matt 19:8–9). Here, once more, I found myself admiring the man, all the more so regretting the bad blood between him and the Pharisees, whom I followed.

Reflecting on the cause, it seemed to me that day that Jesus and the Pharisees in common wanted to persuade people in general that the Torah was not so simple, that it required deeper devotion than ordinary folk supposed. This was very much the point of Jesus' profound restatement of some of the Ten Commandments. And in their own way and setting, it also was the point of the Pharisees' "traditions of the elders," their special rules. No wonder Jesus told people his burden was light, but theirs was heavy; what he asked of others he did himself; what they asked of others they didn't do themselves. Here is his competition:

"Woe to you, scribes and Pharisees, hypocrites! for you traverse sea and land to make a single proselyte, and when he becomes a proselyte, you make him twice as much a child of hell as yourselves." (Matt 23:15)

No wonder the bad blood. Here was a man constantly in motion, walking the paths of the country, trying to win disciples and teach his message, and out there are teachers ("rabbis") competing with him for the very same people. His message to them was, you have nothing to give people. And we can only imagine their message to him.

Well, who won that day? From the remarks of Jesus, it seemed to me that he thought he had quite an opponent with which to contend:

> "Woe to you, scribes and Pharisees, hypocrites! for you are like whitewashed tombs, which outwardly appear beautiful, but within they are full of dead men's bones and all uncleanness. So you also outwardly appear righteous to men, but within, you are full of hypocrisy and iniquity." (Matt 23:27–28)

When I heard him make these remarks, I could not but wonder whether this master found the other side weighty competition indeed, if he could concede that, to third parties, "they appear beautiful." "You look righteous to men," but you're hypocrites.

If we ask ourselves what is at stake in this awful argument, we have to recall two simple facts. The first concerns the Pharisees, the second, Jesus. The Pharisees are people who want Israel to be holy. As we're going to see in the next chapter, this had some very particular meanings then, and it still does today. But, it is clear, in the Pharisees' view, to keep the Ten Commandments and the Golden Rule is to obey God's most fundamental commandment to Israel: "You shall be holy; for I the Lord your God am holy." And Jesus maintained that holiness was a sham: For the sake of your tradition, you have made void the word of God.

Then what does Jesus offer instead of a life of holiness "like God"? It would carry us far afield to give a full answer to that question; twenty centuries of Christians have debated it. But if I had to point to one thing to which Jesus would surely point, it is the kingdom of heaven, which, he held, was soon to come into being. Over and over again, Jesus tried to explain what was at stake: "Repent, for the kingdom of heaven is at hand" was Jesus' first message (Matt 4:17). So at stake is overcoming sin, so as to enter God's kingdom. Jesus preached the gospel of the kingdom and healed every disease and infirmity (Matt 9:35). Over and over again, he explained what was on his mind in parables, and these, time and again, concerned the kingdom of heaven, what it is like, how it is to be understood.

One day, for example, I heard the master give three parables, each of them pointing toward the same conclusion:

"The kingdom of heaven is like treasure hidden in a field, which a man found and covered up; then in his joy, he goes and sells all that he has and buys that field.

"Again, the kingdom of heaven is like a merchant in search of fine pearls, who, on finding one pearl of great value, went and sold all that he had and bought it.

"Again, the kingdom of heaven is like a net which was thrown into the sea and gathered fish of every kind; when it was full, men drew it ashore and sat down and sorted the good into vessels but threw away the bad. So it will be at the close of the age. The angels will come out and separate the evil from the righteous, and throw them into the furnace of fire; there men will weep and gnash their teeth.

"Have you understood all this?"

They said to him, "Yes."

And he said, "Therefore every scribe who has been trained for the kingdom of heaven is like a householder who brings out of his treasure what is new and what is old." (Matt 13:44–52)

Among the many important teachings of the master, the ones concerning the kingdom of heaven take pride of place. And they hold together many of the others: for example, the one that struck me as so uncompromising, to sell all I have to follow the master.

By itself, the saying stood in stunning contrast with the teachings of the Torah. But joined with the teaching of the kingdom of heaven, which is coming soon, that saying, like many others, forms part of a coherent message.

But it is a message the Pharisees are not hearing, because they have a different message. And it is one that scarcely intersects with the teaching of Jesus. His is a message of forgiveness of sin in the here and now, in preparation for the coming of the kingdom of heaven in the on-rushing future. The Pharisees' is a message of purification for a life of holiness in the here and now.

Faced with the choice – Jesus or the Pharisees – I would have honored the one, but followed the other. I would honor Jesus, but I would follow the Pharisees, and I do that even now: it's why I wrote this book. For the Torah had defined Israel as a kingdom of priests and a holy people. That is the way taken by the Pharisees. Their Israel found commonality in a shared, holy way of life, required of all Israelites – so Scripture held. The Mosaic Torah defined that way of life in both cultic and moral terms, and the prophets laid great stress on the latter. What made Israel holy – its way of life, its moral character – depended primarily on how people lived. And that was in the here and now. What the Pharisees had to say about what would happen later on, Jesus never suggests; that is not a point on which he had an argument with them.

But in retrospect, we wonder how much of an argument the two sides had anyhow. For Pharisees were a group shaped by the holy way of life of Israel, talking about sanctification. Jesus and his disciples were a group concerned with sin and atonement in preparation for the near-term coming of God's kingdom. The two neither converse nor argue.

When I walked home that afternoon, I began to suspect that Jesus and the Pharisees – including me – really were just different people talking about different things to different people. Yet, as is clear, neither group could avoid recognizing the other. What kept taking place, as we'll see in the next chapter, really was not a discussion, let alone a debate, but only a confrontation of people with nothing in common pursuing programs of discourse that did not in any way intersect. Not much of an argument.

But as I thought about it, I realized that there was a reason: sanctification addresses one set of human concerns, salvation, a different set. And the reason the two sides could not argue was that neither was talking about what was of interest to the other.

Sanctification categorically requires the designation of what is holy against what is not holy. To sanctify is to set apart. No sanctification can encompass everyone or leave no room for someone in particular to be holy. One need not be "holier than thou," but the *holy* requires the contrary category, the *not-holy*. The kingdom of Heaven, coming soon, has nothing to do with this; what is at issue is gaining entry into God's kingdom. So, once more, how can two groups – Jesus' disciples, the Pharisees – understand one another when one raises the issue of the sanctification, and the other the salvation? Again – so the thought kept running through my mind – really no argument, but just different people talking about different things to different people.

Well, then, was I ready to write off one side or the other? Just because I could not follow Jesus, did that mean I had to suppose not that I'd walked away from him, but that he'd walked out on Israel's Torah?

Well, that depends. On the one side, I could see that the Torah had room for three kinds of true teachers: priests, sages, and prophets. The priests call upon writings such as important passages of Moses' Torah: Exodus, Leviticus, Numbers, and Deuteronomy; they tell about God's kingdom. The sages call upon writings such as Proverbs and Qohelet [Ecclesiastes], a tradition of wisdom to be taught by learned persons. And the prophets of today could refer to the prophets of old, as Jesus constantly did: Isaiah and Jeremiah, but also Ezekiel and the twelve.

How did each of these three figures, with a rich heritage in the Torah of Moses, see the world?

The priest viewed society as organized along structural lines emanating from the Temple. His caste stood at the top of a social scale in which all things were properly organized, each with its correct name and proper place. The inherent sanctity of the people of Israel, through the priests' genealogy, came to its richest embodiment in the high priest. Food set apart for the priests' rations, at God's command, possessed the same sanctity; so, too, did the table at which priests ate. To the priest, for the sacred society of Israel, history was an account of what happened in, and (alas) on occasions to, the Temple.

To the sage, the life of society demanded wise regulations. Relationships among people required guidance by the laws enshrined in the Torah and best interpreted by scribes; the task of Israel was to construct a way of life in accordance with the revealed rules of the Torah. The sage, master of the rules, stood at the head.

Prophecy insisted that the fate of the nation depended upon the faith and moral condition of society, a fact to which Israel's internal and external history testified. Both sage and priest saw Israel from the viewpoint of eternity, but the nation had to live out its life in this world, among other peoples coveting the very same land, and within the context of Roman imperial policies and politics. The messiah's kingship would resolve the issue of Israel's subordinate relationship to other nations and empires, establishing once and for all the desirable, correct context for priest and sage alike.

The priest perceived the Temple as the center of the world: beyond it he saw in widening circles the less holy, then the unholy, and further still, the unclean. All lands outside the Land of Israel were unclean with corpse uncleanness; all other peoples were unclean just as corpses were unclean. Accordingly, in the world, life abided within Israel; and in Israel, within the Temple. Outside, in the far distance, were vacant lands and dead peoples, comprising an undifferentiated wilderness of death – a world of uncleanness.

From such a perspective, no teaching about Israel among the nations, no interest in the history of Israel and its meaning, was apt to emerge.

The wisdom of the sage pertained in general to the streets, marketplaces, and domestic establishments (the household units) of Israel. What the sage said was wisdom as much for gentiles as for Israel. The universal wisdom proved international, moving easily across the boundaries of culture and language, from eastern to southern to western Asia. It focused, by definition, upon human experience common to all and undifferentiated by nation, essentially unaffected by the large movements of history. Wisdom spoke about fathers and sons, masters and disciples, families and villages, not about nations, armies, and destiny.

Because of their very diversity, these three principal modes of Israelite existence might easily cohere. Each focused on a particular aspect of the national life, and none essentially contradicted any other. One could worship at the Temple, study the Torah, and fight in the army of the Messiah – and some did all three. Yet we must see these modes of being – and their consequent forms of piety – as separate. Each contained its own potentiality to achieve full realization without reference to the others. But that is not how life works. We cannot split up our village into the priests' neighborhood, the prophets' neighborhood, and the sages' neighborhood. We are one village. Jesus and his disciples lay heavy stress on teachings of the prophets, because Jesus is teaching the disciples – and all Israel he wants as his disciples – how to prepare for the coming of God's rule, which is near at hand. So he speaks of the forgiveness of sin and atonement at the end of days, which is upon us. The Pharisees lay heavy stress on teachings of the priests in Leviticus and want Israel to live now, here and everywhere, in accord with those rules that the Torah of Moses set forth for the sanctification of the priests. We really do conflict, because we agree: the one calls for salvation at the end of time, the other, sanctification in the here and now. How are we going to live together?

Well, for one thing, much depends on humble matters. And here, there really is a point of contention between Jesus and us Pharisees. For as I said at the outset, I believe in Judaism now and so identify with the Pharisees then. Is the kingdom of God in the here and now? Or only in the coming future? And where, and how, and under what circumstances do I serve God and live the Godly life? Or to put matters in humble terms: Does God care about what I eat for breakfast?

8

The Road from Capernaum

"Many will come from east and west and sit at table with Abraham, Isaac, and Jacob in the kingdom of heaven, while the sons of the kingdom will be thrown into the outer darkness; there men will weep and gnash their teeth." And to the centurion Jesus said, "Go, be it done for you as you have believed." And the servant was healed at that very moment.

Matt. 8:5–13

When Jesus came down from the mountain, with great crowds following (Mt. 8:1), he headed toward Capernaum. I caught up with him, swept along in the happy, but strangely quiet throngs. Serene silence prevailed, everyone was thinking about the remarkable message of the master: the kingdom of Heaven goes to the poor in spirit, the meek shall inherit the earth, the pure in heart shall see God. With teachings such as these, with this torah, with the rest I found myself exalted, encountering the sublime. But I knew that I should not be following the master much longer. What I heard at the Mount was necessary but not sufficient for loving God with all my heart and soul and might and living in God's dominion here and now. The silence bore its own eloquent message: what he did not say upon his Sinai. But I did not know that, within that very day, when we got to Capernaum, he would fill in the silence with an eloquent gesture, and everything would be clear.

That would happen presently. Here and now, though, Jesus spied me out before I saw him and motioned to me to join him on the way, which I did.

I waited for him to speak, but he kept silent, and so did I. But in my silence, walking by his side, I reflected, "Like Moses on Mount Sinai, so Jesus has come down from Heaven and taught torah. Among those to whom he speaks – the poor in spirit, the mourners, the meek, those who hunger and thirst for righteousness, the merciful, the pure in heart, the peace makers – I look in vain for that very 'you' to whom Moses speaks, that 'you' whom God brought forth from the Land of Egypt, from the house of bondage: Israel."

After a while, in the penetrating silence, he looked at me and said, "You're wondering about the 'you' to whom I speak, about Israel."

"Yes, I am."

"True, on the mount I said nothing of Israel, when I blessed the poor in spirit and those who mourn and all the others."

"No, you said nothing."

"Wait."

More silence.

We walked on. I waited.

As he entered Capernaum, a centurion came forward to him, beseeching him and saying, "Lord, my servant is lying paralyzed at home" And he said to him, "I will come and heal him." But the centurion answered him, "Lord, I am not worthy to have you come under my roof, but only say the word and my servant will be healed. For I am a man under authority, with soldiers under me, and I say to one, 'Go,' and he goes, and to another, 'Come,' and he comes, and to my slave, 'Do this,' and he does it." When Jesus heard him, he marveled and said to those who followed him, "Truly I say to you, not even in Israel have I found such faith. I tell you, many will come from east and west and sit at table with Abraham, Isaac, and Jacob in the kingdom of heaven, while the sons of the kingdom will be thrown into the outer darkness; there men will weep and gnash their teeth." And to the centurion Jesus said, "Go, be it done for you as you have believed." And the servant was healed at that very moment. (Matt. 8:5–13)

I marveled at the mighty miracle. Believing was easy. I had heard of holy men's doing such miracles: how their prayers brought healing to distant patients. Honi the Circle-Drawer would do no less. I found no difficulty in accepting what my own eyes saw and my own ears heard. But all the more, I wondered at the master's silence. So, as Jesus turned to go to Peter's house (Mt. 8:14), I asked for a moment of the master's time and he granted it.

"I too believe, master, that in time to come, many will come from east and west and sit at table with the patriarchs and matriarchs in the kingdom of Heaven. The prophets say no less. But that will come about because they accept God's unity and the Torah in which they are taught God's rule. But the Torah tells me nothing about how the children of the Kingdom will be thrown into outer darkness.

"And just now, yesterday, on the Mount, your eloquence in speech found its match in silence: what you did not say concerns me. Where, in your torah on the Mount, is there a message for the already-faithful, the already-citizens, of God's kingdom?

"Much that I hear from the Mountain is necessary. But the message is insufficient. You leave out too much. And that concerns me."

With patience he accepted my concern, understanding the act of engagement as a commitment too.

"What do I leave out?"

"Three things. First, you do not tell me the story of the Torah, which tells about beginnings and endings, where we come from, who we are. Second, you do not tell me about us, Israel. Third, you do not account for the unfaith of the gentiles."

"The centurion believed."

"In you. Does that make him us, Israel, and has that faith fulfilled the requirements of the Torah?"

"Then tell me your story."

The story that I had to tell is not my story, it is the story told by Moses in the Torah and the other prophets too. It is the story of the creation and fall of Man and what God has done to repair the world. Here is that story that the Hebrew Scriptures teach. I listened in vain in the torah at the Mountain for echoes of that story. Those silences – what Jesus did not say on the mountain – bear an eloquent message, brought to actuality in the encounter with the centurion. The gentile's faith not only wins him a place at the table, it also condemns to outer darkness some whose faith has also placed them at the table.

But to be Israel is to know and love the one and only God who made the world. That is because God brought Israel into being to do right what Adam had done wrong, willingly to accept God's will. The Torah and the prophets tell the story of God's quest for Eden once more, now to be realized by those who accept the heritage and inheritance and become the children of Abraham and Sarah and so form Israel at Sinai.

Moses begins his story at Eden, but Jesus on the mountain tells no story at all. The initial exposition of how things are, set forth in Genesis, tells how God made the world, recognized his failure in doing so and corrected it. Through Abraham and Sarah a new humanity came into being, ultimately to meet God at Sinai and to record the meeting in the Torah. But then the question arises, what of the rest of humanity, the children of Noah but not of the sector of the family beginning with Abraham and Sarah? The simple logic of the story responds: the rest of humanity, outside the holy family and beyond the commanding voice of Sinai, does not know God but worships idols. These are what we call "the gentiles." And the gentiles, not Israel, govern the world. That is Scripture's story, and that also is the story sages tell. But on the Mountain Jesus tells no story, and in Capernaum he welcomes the centurion to the table of the Kingdom because of faith in himself alone.

"Here, master, is my story of who is Israel in relationship to everybody else, and of what that faith of Israel consists. It is how God meets the nations, and Israel among them, and what happened that day that forms the counterpart to today in Capernaum."

Sifré to Deuteronomy CCCXLIII:IV.1ff.:

1. A. Another teaching concerning the phrase, "He said, 'The Lord came from Sinai'":

B. When the Omnipresent appeared to give the Torah to Israel, it was not to Israel alone that he revealed himself but to every nation.

C. First of all he came to the children of Esau. He said to them, "Will you accept the Torah?"

D. They said to him, "What is written in it?"

E. He said to them, "'You shall not murder'" (Ex. 20:13).

F. They said to him, "The very being of 'those men' [namely, us] and of their father is to murder, for it is said, 'But the hands are the hands of Esau'"(Gen. 27:22). 'By your sword you shall live'" (Gen. 27:40).

G. So he went to the children of Ammon and Moab and said to them, "Will you accept the Torah?"

H. They said to him, "What is written in it?"

I. He said to them, "'You shall not commit adultery'" (Ex. 20:13).

J. They said to him, "The very essence of fornication belongs to them [us], for it is said, 'Thus were both the daughters of Lot with child by their fathers'" (Gen. 19:36).

K. So he went to the children of Ishmael and said to them, "Will you accept the Torah?"

L. They said to him, "What is written in it?"

M. He said to them, "'You shall not steal'" (Ex. 20:13).

N. They said to him, "The very essence of their [our] father is thievery, as it is said, 'And he shall be a wild ass of a man'" (Gen. 16:12).

O. And so it went. He went to every nation, asking them, "Will you accept the Torah?"

P. For so it is said, "All the kings of the earth shall give you thanks, O Lord, for they have heard the words of your mouth" (Ps. 138:4).

Q. Might one suppose that they listened and accepted the Torah?

R. Scripture says, "And I will execute vengeance in anger and fury upon the nations, because they did not listen" (Mic. 5:14).

S. And it is not enough for them that they did not listen, but even the seven religious duties that the children of Noah indeed accepted upon themselves they could not uphold before breaking them.

T. When the Holy One, blessed be He, saw that that is how things were, he gave them to Israel.

"Now master, may I tell you a parable, involving not a king but a common person:"

2. A. The matter may be compared to the case of a person who sent his ass and dog to the threshing floor and loaded up a *letekh* of grain on his ass and three *seahs* of grain on his dog. The ass went along, while the dog panted.

B. He took a seah of grain off the dog and put it on the ass, so with the second, so with the third.

C. Thus was Israel: they accepted the Torah, complete with all its secondary amplifications and minor details, even the seven religious duties that the children of Noah could not uphold without breaking them did the Israelites come along and accept.

D. That is why it is said, "The Lord came from Sinai; he shone upon them from Seir."

"So, master, I listen to what you do not say, honoring and affirming much of what you do set forth. And I find much necessary, but – now perhaps you may understand why – the whole insufficient, by the criterion of the Torah of Moses set forth at Sinai."

Silence. But a bit later on, as we yet walked together, I would hear his response to my question, what of Israel? For, true teacher that he was, he had listened carefully to my question and had thought about it. He entered my mind as I tried to enter his. But, like a true teacher, he also took for granted that I knew how to listen and respond. So his reply came not to me and not in the setting of my inquiry, but, rather, in his instructions to another disciple – was it Peter? – asking another question altogether, namely, permission to go and bury his father, his patrimony.

We were leaving Capernaum. Before going with the master on the way, the disciple asked:

"Lord, let me first go and bury my father."

But Jesus said to him, "Follow me, and leave the dead to bury their own dead" (Mt. 8:21–22).

So much for the patrimony and the heritage of Israel: death, for the dead themselves to bury.

"But," so I thought when I heard those words, "to us, Israel, our fathers and our mothers never die: Abraham, Isaac, Jacob, Sarah, Rebecca, Rachel and Leah live in our prayers and they live in the Torah and so they live in us. Would the master deny that, and would his disciples – Israel all! – not understand?

"But above all, what would the centurion, sitting at the table in the Kingdom of Heaven with Abraham, Isaac, and Jacob – what would he have made of his dinner companions?"

But these questions I did not ask. From Capernaum, Jesus went his way. And I knew where I should go: to village and to home, to God's kingdom in the here and now.

9

You Shall Tithe All the Yield of Your Seed

vs

You Tithe Mint and Dill and Cumin and Have Neglected the Weightier Matters of the Law

"Woe to you, scribes and Pharisees, hypocrites! for you tithe mint and dill and cumin and have neglected the weightier matters of the law, justice and mercy and faith; these you ought to have done, without neglecting the others. You blind guides, straining out a gnat and swallowing a camel!"

Matthew 23:23–24

"Woe to you, scribes and Pharisees, hypocrites! for you cleanse the outside of the cup and of the plate, but inside they are full of extortion and rapacity. You blind Pharisee! first cleanse the inside of the cup and of the plate, that the outside also may be clean."

Matthew 23:25–26

Moses says, "You shall tithe all the yield of your seed" (Deut 14:22); and Jesus says, do that but don't neglect more important things. No one doubts that there are more important things, for instance, "Love your neighbor as yourself" and "You shall be holy." But part of holiness is tithing, along with the other teachings of the Torah. No one would claim that everything is as important as everything else; and everyone would agree with Jesus: Do the major commandments – the Ten Commandments, for instance – without neglecting the lesser ones.

But Jesus takes for granted that right conflicts with rite. He repeatedly draws a contrast between inner corruption and outer piety, or between inner uncleanness and external signs of cleanness. True, he concedes, tithing is part of the Torah. But if you tithe but neglect "weightier matters of the law," then you are "blind guides." The remarkable saying of Rabbi Pinhas ben Yair – "… holiness leads to modesty, modesty leads to the fear of sin, the fear of sin leads to piety, piety leads to the Holy Spirit …" – calls into question the certainty that we are one thing or another: either pious or moral.

So one day I formulated my question: "But what if you tithe but also do justice, love mercy, and faithfully affirm God's rule? Is that what you really want of me?" Because, sir, if it is, then I can make sense of your message, concerning the kingdom of Heaven, in the framework of what the Torah has already instructed me to do and believe.

But if not – God forbid! For then if not, how shall I keep eternal Israel's enduring commitment? So any teaching today has to come under the judgment of that ancient oath: "We shall do and we shall obey." If I can stand loyally by that oath, then, but only then, I can come to terms with any teacher's message for Israel.

Anyhow, that is the question I wanted to ask – an argument, an ultimatum really.

But I didn't get to ask it, because I didn't have to. In fact, as I listened on the fringes of the crowd, I found my own reply. For the answer to that question is signaled in the next statement: "You cleanse the outside of the cup and of the plate, but inside they are full of extortion and rapacity." The sense of the saying is that if you are not clean inside, then the outside may look clean but isn't. This reminds us of precisely that same contrast – inner corruption vs. external piety – that Jesus draws in the same context: "you are like whitewashed tombs, which outwardly appear beautiful, but within they are full of dead men's bones and all uncleanness." So he sees a conflict between rite and right – people good at rite aren't terribly interested in morality.

But while many share that prejudice, many more find self-evident the prophet's denunciation of those who are ritualistic but unrighteous, for instance, the prophet Nathan's confrontation with King David: "Have you murdered and also inherited?" or Amos' contention that those who sell the needy in exchange for a pair of shoes can never be right with God. And when we affirm the prophetic insistence on right, we also affirm that rite must lead to right, and that the purpose of doing the commandments, as the Talmud says, "is to purify the human heart." So there is a place in God's scheme for rite and also right, though of course what God most wants of us is righteousness.

But in my village I would have known plenty of people who obey the commandments of the Sabbath and of loving neighbor as self, and who see no conflict between them: they all represent the will of the living God, stated in one and the same place, the Torah, through the mediation of one and the same prophet, Moses. And in the world of living Judaism today I know hosts of people who respond to the moral as much as to the ritual commandments, and whose lives really do provide us with examples in the flesh of what the Torah wants us to be.

Well, then, I wonder, hearing these strong words, does Jesus really care about the dietary laws of the Torah? And one of his disciples told me a saying – I wasn't around that day – that settled the question:

And he called the people to him and said to them, "Hear and understand: not what goes into the mouth defiles a man, but what comes out of the mouth, this defiles a man … Do you not see that whatever goes into the mouth passes into the stomach and so passes on? But what comes out of the mouth proceeds from the heart, and this defiles a man. For out of the heart come evil thoughts, murder, adultery, fornication, theft, false witness, slander. These are what defile a man; but to eat with unwashed hands does not defile a man." (Matt 15:10, 17–20)

So maybe I was wrong earlier. I conceded too much, too soon. For Jesus there is no conflict between rite and right, because in his opinion, rites are null; rituals mean nothing; all that matters is obedience to the moral and ethical teachings of the Torah.

If what I eat does not make me "unclean" (a term I'll explain in a moment), then the rules of the Torah about what to eat and what not to eat are null. Jesus makes his position clear, and it is not the one that he took when I first heard him, up on the mountain. In drawing a contrast between right and rite and saying that eating with unwashed hands doesn't mean a thing, or what you eat doesn't make you unclean, then he has abolished some of the dots and iotas of the Torah.

So the master makes it clear that there really is a contrast to be drawn between the commandments that tell us to love our neighbor as ourselves and the commandments that tell us about eating and drinking. Yet, my respect for the man is such that I hesitate to conclude he has said one thing in one place, and a contradictory thing in some other. So I conclude that I really don't understand him. He sees a conflict where I don't, and I see God's will to be done, where he doesn't.

But that leads me to wonder once again, do we mean the same thing at all when we speak of such matters? For my understanding of eating with unwashed hands, tithing even dill and cumin, washing plates and cups, is such that I see no point of intersection – let alone tension and conflict – between right and rite. When Jesus says, "these you ought to have done, without neglecting the others," as when he insisted, "till heaven and earth pass away, not an iota, not a dot, will pass from the Torah until all is accomplished," how he squares these true-to-the-Torah teachings with the invidious comparisons he draws between uncleanness and immorality is not entirely clear to me.

Now, as a matter of fact, the Torah devotes much attention to food. Right from the story of creation onward, one important focus is on what people eat. The Garden of Eden is an orchard; Noah offered up sacrifices of animals; all the patriarchs of Israel did the same. So a subject about which, as a matter of fact, Matthew's Jesus has very little to say – and nothing affirmative at that – occupies a considerable position in the Torah's narrative and law.

First of all, Israel serves God by offering up animal sacrifices as well as grain, wine, and other produce of the Holy Land. So in the Torah one form of divine service – sacrifice – takes the earthly form of food. It did not have to be that way; one may offer God a gift of flowers, or incense, or the gesture of a sacred dance, for example. But the Torah wants food. Second, the priesthood is supplied with food as well. The priests get a share of the sacrifices in the Temple. They also stand in for God, who owns the Holy Land, and God's share of the crop is set aside for the priests and Levites as well as for the poor and indigent. Third, all Israel is instructed on certain foods that may not be eaten as "unclean," and others that may be eaten. So these are not concerns that the Pharisees have made up for themselves, not at all. In fact, how life is sustained – through raising crops and herds in the Holy Land – forms one central issue in the Torah's conception of the life of the kingdom of priests and the holy people.

Well, what about this matter of "purity"? When it comes to considerations of purity, the Torah is explicit that, when they come to the Temple courtyard to do their holy work, the priests and others who work with them, including the people as a whole, are to be "pure." The word "pure" translates the Hebrew word *tahor* and "impure" translates *tamé*. But the meaning of "purity" in context is not conveyed by that translation. We think of "pure" in very general terms. But in the Torah, "pure" and "impure" in the main refer to a particular context, and that is the Temple and its service to God. When something is called "pure," in general it is acceptable to the holy rite, and if it is "impure," it is not. So the word "pure" in this context has a very limited and particular meaning indeed. In fact, an alternative translation for "pure" in many contexts would be "acceptable in the holy place," and "impure," "unacceptable."

We find we have moved quite a distance from where we began – which is the contrast between "inner" and "outer" purity. Indeed, in this setting – when we're talking about the holy Temple, which Moses described and which in later times Israel built in the holy land – "purity" is simply not a category that has anything to do with ethics. Not only is there no tension between rite and right, there is no point of intersection. Contrasting "inner" impurity with "outer" purity, meaning an unethical private life joined to a ritually correct external life, is incomprehensible.

The issue of "purity" does not concern ethics, does not intersect with ethics, and does not stand in tension with ethics when one has attained "acceptability in the holy place" even though guilty of a lack of mercy. Why not? Because what makes one acceptable in the holy place is one set of considerations, while what makes the same person morally upright or unacceptable is simply another set of considerations. In contemporary terms, we cannot say that because a surgeon is "pure" for the operating room but guilty of fornicating with her lab assistant, therefore she is a "hypocrite." In very simple terms, one thing has absolutely nothing to do with the other (unless the lab assistant has hepatitis or AIDS).

So what about this "purity" meaning "acceptability for the Temple and its cult"? Precisely what this means is set forth in the books of Leviticus and Numbers. Sources of uncleanness are spelled out at Leviticus 12–15 and elsewhere. If I had to say in a few words what makes something unclean, it is something that, for one reason or another, is abnormal, disrupts the economy of nature or society. Take the corpse, for example, as at Numbers 19:1ff. Death disturbs the house of life by releasing corpse uncleanness. Then there are, as specified at Leviticus 12–15, menstrual blood, flux of blood outside of the menstrual cycle, and a flow from the penis outside of the normal reproductive process. Here, too, the source of the uncleanness is constituted by that which functions contrary to nature or which disrupts what is deemed to be the normal course of nature.

The bed and the table are to be so preserved as to remain within the normal lines of the natural economy. It follows that cleanness of the table is to be attained and protected, with regard to both the food which is consumed thereon and to the utensils used in preparing and serving it. What is ordinary, useful, distinctive to a given purpose, and normal is deemed susceptible to uncleanness and must therefore be kept apart from those things which, for their own reasons, are deemed extraordinary and abnormal. If such an object then is made unclean, it must be restored to cleanness through natural processes.

These readings of the Torah's rules are not the only way to understand why what is unclean is classified in that way; they are just a way of suggesting that in matters of cleanness and uncleanness, food that we eat and food we do not eat, washing hands to rid them of uncleanness and washing dishes for the same purpose, we are not engaged in actions that have any bearing on ethics, but on the other hand, these things do matter. Not everything matters because it has a bearing on right action, on ethics, even on human relationships. Some things matter because they bear on our relationship with God, and while that involves loving our neighbor as ourself, it also requires us to try to be "holy" because God is holy; and in the Torah, holiness bears very concrete and specific meanings, not all of them having to do with human relationships by any means.

We have wandered a long way from our starting point, my argument with Jesus on whether or not we have to contrast right and rite. It is part of my larger argument, begun two chapters ago, on what really counts: "You shall be holy, for I the Lord your God am holy," vs. "If you would be perfect, go, sell all you have and come, follow me." If you do not have a clear picture of the requirements of being holy as the Torah lays them out, you are never going to understand why if I were there, I would not have followed him.

For I am deeply troubled by what I conceive to be Jesus' rejection of what is fundamental to the Torah. I don't mean some niggling details, such as engage us here; I mean the main point of it all: Either "be holy, for I the Lord am holy" or "if you would be perfect ... follow me." For me, being holy has been defined by the Torah; it is the only way I know what God means by holiness, following the Ten Commandments, for instance. So we have to pursue this issue where it leads, this question of sanctification.

The particular point of consequence, for the Torah, that makes the purity laws important pertains in the main to the Temple and the priesthood. To explain, let me ask a simple question: What, in accord with the law of the Torah, can I do if I am pure, but not do if I am not pure? The answer is mainly, if I am pure, I can come to the Temple; if I am not pure, I cannot. That is not the only answer, but it is the principal one. Then who has to be pure? In the books of the Torah – Leviticus, Numbers, and Deuteronomy – it is the priesthood that has to be pure, when they come to perform their holy service in the Temple. People other than priests have to be pure when they come to the Temple, for example, on a pilgrim festival, such as Passover, Pentecost, or Tabernacles.

But there is one further point. When priests eat their share of the offerings of the altar, or when at home they eat the rations that the people set aside from their crops, they have to be in a state of cultic acceptability, that is, "pure" in this very sense in which the Torah uses the word.

Well, then, why in the world would the Pharisees have cared whether anybody washed hands before meals, or plates and cups and all the rest? The priests are explicitly told two things. First of all, not only they but also their families at home may eat the Holy Things that the people of Israel give to the Lord. And second, they are told, when they eat these Holy Things, they are not to be "unclean," in the very distinctive sense I have now spelled out:

> And the Lord said to Moses, "Tell Aaron and his sons ... If any one of all your descendants throughout your generations approaches the holy things, which the people of Israel dedicate to the Lord, while he has an uncleanness, that person shall be cut off from my presence: I am the Lord. None of the line of Aaron who is a leper or suffers a discharge may eat of the Holy Things until he is clean. Whoever touches anything that is unclean through contact with the dead or a man who has had an emission of semen, and whoever touches a creeping thing by which men may be made unclean, or a man from whom he may take uncleanness, whatever his uncleanness may be – the person who touches any such shall be unclean until the evening and shall not eat of the Holy Things unless he has bathed his body in water. When the sun is down, he shall be clean; and afterward he may eat of the holy things, because such are his food." (Lev 22:2–7)

Now the story becomes very simple. These rules apply not only in the Temple, where the priests eat their share of the Holy Things of the altar. They also apply to the priests' wives and children, and that must be, at home as well.

What has all this to do with the Pharisees? Well, clearly, Jesus takes for granted that Pharisees consider the purity and food rules to apply outside the Temple and (assuming not all Pharisees were priests) outside of the priesthood. He presupposes that fact, and it is one of the foundations of his criticism of their ways. He says in so many words that it is not "the tradition of the elders" at all for people to wash their hands when they eat. But why should people wash their hands when they eat if they are not priests in the Temple or at home preparing to eat their holy rations? He says his disciples don't have to wash hands, because eating everyday food doesn't require adhering to the purity rules; these pertain to the cult, and the Torah is clear on that point. Any other view he classifies as merely "the tradition of the elders," not part of the Torah at all.

Of course he is right; nothing in the Torah suggests that I eat in a state of cultic acceptability everyday food, food that has no place in the Temple as an offering, food that is not a gift to the priesthood, for instance. Then when I do maintain that eating everyday food as though it were Temple or priests' food, eating at home as though I were in the Temple, conducting myself, an ordinary person, as if I were a priest – when I do these things, what am I saying through such actions?

The answer, it seems to me, is clear and simple: I am acting out the rites of sanctification of the Temple and the priesthood. So I am pretending that every place in the holy land is as holy as the Temple. I am acting as if every Israelite were a priest. I am so behaving as if to say that my everyday food at home is subject to the same rules of "purity" ("cultic acceptability") as the priest's holy food in the Temple. In all of these ways, what am I doing?

I am responding to the commandment of holiness. This is what the Torah means when it says, "You shall be holy; for I the Lord your God am holy," and it is what God said in so many words to Moses:

"You have seen what I did to the Egyptians, and how I bore you on eagles' wings and brought you to myself. Now therefore, if you will obey my voice and keep my covenant, you shall be my own possession among all peoples; for all the earth is mine, and you shall be to me a kingdom of priests and a holy nation." (Exod 19:4–6)

So, the point is, when I keep these rules, which the Torah lays down for the holy place, I act as though every place is holy. When I eat my meals in accord with the rules that govern the priests when they eat holy food, I am acting as though I were a priest and as though my food came from the altar. It is one way of being holy, one way of acting out what it means to be a kingdom of priests and a holy people.

Here is an everyday way of reading the Torah, a way that takes very seriously the Torah's insistence that God cares what Israel eats, what I eat for breakfast, in the humble way in which I put matters just now. This is a way of living a holy life that is perpetual and constant, always here and now, always relevant to this morning's most immediate concerns. I am always in motion through the confluence and contrast of opposites perpetually moving from the one side to the other – from the clean to the unclean, from the unclean to the clean. Death happens constantly. Water for purification flows regularly from heaven to earth. The source of menstrual uncleanness is as regular as the rain. Meals happen day by day, and if for the Israelite, the table is a regular resort, so too is the bed. The Torah's life of holiness therefore creates an unchanging rhythm of its own. It is based on recurrent natural sources of uncleanness and perpetual sources of cleanness, and it focuses upon the loci of ordinary life in which people, whatever else they do, invariably and always are going to be engaged: nourishment and reproduction – *the sustenance of life and the creation of life*. What God wants of me is to create and sustain life in accord with the rules of the Torah.

For in the end, in the Torah one important opposite of *unclean* is *holy*. Israel's natural condition, pertinent to the three dimensions of life – Land, people, and cult – is holiness. God's people are to be like God in order to have access to him. Accordingly, it is what causes Israel to cease to be holy, in the present context uncleanness, which is abnormal, and to state the reverse, what is abnormal is unclean. Cleanness thus is a this-worldly expression of the conception of the holiness and the set-apartness of all three – people, Land, and cult.

By keeping oneself apart from what affects and afflicts other lands, peoples, and cults ("the Canaanites who were here before you"), the Israelite attains that separateness which is expressive of holiness and reaches the holiness which is definitive also of the natural condition of Israel. The processes of nature correspond to those of supernature, restoring in this world the datum to which this world corresponds. The disruptive sources of uncleanness – unclean foods and creeping things that have died, persons who depart from their natural condition in sexual and reproductive organs (or later on, in their skin condition and physical appearance), and the corpse – all of these affect Israel and necessitate restorative natural processes.

So it seems to me the Pharisees are saying when they do these odd rites of theirs. And if that is what is at stake, then the issues that separate Jesus from people like the Pharisees, including myself, are not trivial. He does not represent them as trivial, and neither do I. When he considers my interest in eating food by the rules of holiness, that is, in sustaining my life, meal by meal, with God's will in mind, he thinks it absurd: straining out a gnat, swallowing a camel. Can we argue?

All I can say is, "Sir, does not God want us to be holy? And are these not the ways that holiness is defined? True, the Ten Commandments and the Golden Rule take pride of place. But the Torah has more in it than those commandments, and you yourself say to keep them all."

The upshot is that, for the Pharisees, the conception of uncleanness functioned in an entirely different framework from ethics, so that associating uncleanness with sin bore no meaning and made no sense at all. Uncleanness addressed an issue quite distinct from a moral one, which can be proven very simply. For Jesus, "uncleanness" served as a metaphor for evil; for him "cleanness" meant to be clean of sin. Baptism, then, was to remove sin. For the Pharisees, "uncleanness" served as a metaphor for not-holy, and for them, "cleanness" served as a metaphor for sanctification. The washing of hands or of persons was to remove uncleanness.

These really are not the same thing. For Jesus, clean or unclean meant virtuous or sinful; hence cleanness is a moral category. It says what kind of person you are. For the Pharisees, clean or unclean meant able to go to the holy Temple or not able to go to the holy Temple. It says what kind of place you can go to, what kind of deed you can do (at that particular moment). But it has no bearing at all on what kind of a person you are or are not. It is not a moral category at all. It describes the state of being in which, at that moment, you find yourself.

We are used to thinking that to be "holier than thou" means to be more virtuous than the other. But that is far from what holiness means and monumentally irrelevant to why holiness is important to me. That is why, as we shall see, representing uncleanness as sin and a sign of wickedness hardly represents a conception generated by the Torah.

This brings us back to the wonderful passage at Mishnah tractate Sotah 9: 15, which shows how cleanness relates to purity and purity to morality or holiness – upward to the coming of the Messiah and the resurrection of the dead:

Heedfulness leads to physical cleanliness, cleanliness to levitical purity, purity to separateness, separateness to holiness, holiness to humility, humility to the shunning of sin, shunning of sin to saintliness, saintliness to the Holy Spirit, the Holy Spirit to the resurrection of the dead.

Clearly, the unclean person is not on that account wicked, and so we cannot contrast uncleanness with morality. The capacity to become clean, a stage on the route to holiness as we saw, finds a counterpart in the capacity to become unclean; the more "holy" something may become, the more susceptible it is to uncleanness.

Can we now formulate issues so that people can discuss the same question, disagree about some one thing? I am inclined to think not. If you think that there is something sinful about uncleanness, then you will find a contrast between cultic cleanness and moral depravity a natural one, a sensible (if invidious) comparison. But if you think that cleanness is not about morality but about the cult, then that comparison is going to make no sense. And at the foundation of the dispute – for it really is a dispute between Jesus and those of us who take our own way and do not choose to follow him – is what makes all the difference. Either the proper conduct of the cult determines the course of the seasons and the prosperity of the Land, or it is "merely ritual" – an unimportant external and not the critical heart.

Jesus preaches the kingdom, the end of time, a moment in very public history, and we who follow the Pharisees focus our attention upon the private establishment of the home and heart. Jesus addresses a one-time, unique *event,* but given the ordinariness of these meals that concern us, the rest of eternal Israel focuses upon "eternity." Our interest is in the recurrent and continuing patterns of life – birth and death, planting and harvest, the regular movement of the sun, moon, stars in heaven, night and day, Sabbaths, festivals, and regular seasons on earth. We share one existential issue: How do we respond to the ups and downs of life?

So if I could respond, in the quiet of a long evening, out of the shouting mobs, and if Jesus cared to listen, what would I say to him?

I would say, "Sir, you and I, all of us who are part of eternal Israel – we really do know the mystery of how to endure through history. Things don't merely *happen* to us Israelites. God makes them happen to teach lessons to Israel. That is what the prophets taught: What happens to us, Israel, takes place because that is a way in which God teaches lessons to us; historical events come about because God wants them to. And we both realize how the prophetic and apocalyptic thinkers in Israel have shaped, reformulated, and interpreted events, treating them as raw material for renewing the life of the group."

So I would point out, perhaps not in so few words, some simple truths. For us, eternal Israel, history is not merely "one damn thing after another." It is important, teaching significant lessons. It had a purpose and was moving somewhere. The writers of Leviticus and Deuteronomy, of the historical books from Joshua through Kings, and of the prophetic literature, agreed that when Israel did God's will, it enjoyed peace, security, and prosperity; when it did not, it was punished at the hands of mighty kingdoms raised up as instruments of God's wrath.

This conception of the meaning of Israel's life produced another question: How long? When would the great events of time come to their climax and conclusion? And as one answer to that question, there arose the hope for the messiah, the anointed of God, who would redeem the people and set them on the right path forever, thus ending the vicissitudes of history.

So I return to my soliloquy, in the quiet of the evening:

"You, sir, ask that question: How long? And you answer it, 'Not long, not long at all.'

"I sir, ask that same question, but all I can offer, by way of an answer, is 'However long – however long, this is what we shall be, what we are called to be: a kingdom of priests and a holy people.'"

And looking back, as we come to the year 2000, I realize it would be very long. But very long, we have sought to remain loyal to our calling: to form a kingdom of priests and a holy people, as God through the Torah of Moses commanded us.

So are we tired of waiting? Some are, most not: patience is a Jewish virtue, and alas, much more often, impatience is a Jewish vice (and it is my vice too). But here let me speak in my own name and say what I stand for: For a Jew, it is a sin to despair. And by our actions, not in times past but in this very day and hour, we have shown and we now show by our life together, by our wanting our life to endure together, that we do not despair. Ours is a people of hope, and we have acted, and act today, in hope.

And to revert to my soliloquy:

"In the meantime, I mean to undertake the quest for eternity in the here and now. You speak of the kingdom of heaven. I hope it comes. But for now, I think we should try to form a society capable of abiding amid change and stress. The nations of the world suppose that they make 'history' and think that their actions matter.

"But God makes history. It is the reality formed in response to God's will that counts as history: God is the King of kings of kings.

"You have your quarrel with the Pharisees, and I don't defend their stupid harassment of you. If I were there that day, I would have protested. But not too much.

"For they do offer an alternative answer to the question that all of us want to address. They do compete with you: they have other questions, other answers, but address the same Israel – and its condition.

"For now, they are out there, acting in their homes as if they were priests in the Temple. If they keep the laws of the priests in the Temple while eating their everyday meals at home, then they are acting at home as though they were priests, engaged in the meals of the Temple. Theirs is a pretense and a sham, but a glorious aspiration: an 'as if' way of life. They lived 'as if' they were priests, 'as if' they had to obey at home the laws that applied to the Temple. So what they then and we now mean is this: to live by the rules that God has set forth for our sanctification. This is what it means to us to be eternal Israel.

"You, sir, speak of the kingdom of heaven, the salvation of Israel. Pharisees, priests, sages – they address the sanctification of Israel. So if we differ on what matters more – salvation at the end of time, or sanctification in the here and now – if that is what is at issue, time will tell; God will settle all these questions – eventually."

"In the meanwhile?"

"Well, in the meanwhile, if you're staying in our village, would you join me for breakfast? Friends?"

"Friends. And yes – I will."

How Much Torah, After All?

"Whoever then relaxes one of the least of these commandments and teaches men so, shall be called least in the kingdom of heaven; but he who does them and teaches them shall be called great in the kingdom of heaven. For I tell you, unless your righteousness exceeds that of the scribes and Pharisees, you will never enter the kingdom of heaven."

Matthew 5:19–20

Over breakfast the next morning, we had a chance to talk; the master planned to leave the village only later in the day. Sitting under a fig tree and enjoying its shade in the morning sun, we looked out over Galilee. He seemed pensive.

I: "Leaving soon?"

He: "Very soon."

"Then what?"

"God knows."

"Jerusalem?"

"Jerusalem."

"O Jerusalem, Jerusalem, killing the prophets and stoning those who are sent to you! How often would I have gathered your children together as a hen gathers her brood under her wings, and you would not! Behold, your house is forsaken and desolate. For I tell you, you will not see me again, until you say, 'Blessed be he who comes in the name of the Lord.'" (Matt 23:37–39)

"Can we still talk about things?"

"So why not?"

I stay silent for a moment, then I turn to him and look him right in the eye: "I honor you, I don't want it said of me, 'A prophet is not without honor except in his own country and in his own house … because of [my] unbelief' (Matt 13:57–8) – I honor you. But my unbelief is not the reason I won't go. Not what I don't believe, which is in you, but what I do believe, which is in the Torah.

"True, I won't go with you to Jerusalem, with your disciples. And I want to explain why. May I?"

Patiently: "You may."

"I really don't see how your teachings and the Torah's teachings come together. That isn't because things you say don't appeal to the Torah; some of them do. It's because most of what you say and most of what the Torah says scarcely intersect.

"To put it simply: You talk about the kingdom of heaven. To me, that means living under the rule of God. The Torah gives us the rules that form the rule of God. And about most of these rules you have very little to say."

"For instance?"

"For instance, Moses tells us to organize a just government, to establish fair and equitable laws. He wants us to choose able men, trustworthy and beyond bribes, to rule the people and judge them (Exod 18:21).

"For instance, Moses tells us how to deal with peoples' fights, with controversy and contention: 'When men quarrel and one strikes the other with a stone ...' (Exod 21:18); 'When a man strikes his slave ...' (Exod 21:20); 'when an ox gores a man or a woman to death ...' (Exod 21:28); 'if a man steals an ox or a sheep, and kills it or sells it ...' (Exod 22:1); 'if a thief is found breaking in, and is struck so that he dies ...' (Exod 22:2); 'when a man causes a field or vineyard to be grazed over, or lets his beast loose and it feeds in another man's field' (Exod 22:5); 'if a man borrows anything of his neighbor, and it is hurt or dies ...' (Exod 22:14); 'if you lend money to any of my people with you who is poor, you shall not be to him as a creditor, and you shall not exact interest from him' (Exod 22:25); and on and on and on.

"Master, I have listened and I have asked, and I have not heard from anyone about how, in the kingdom that you tell us is upon us, we deal with these matters. And there are many others too, about which your silence speaks an eloquent message."

He: "And what might that message be?"

I: "The here and now doesn't matter."

He: "Didn't I say, 'Whoever then relaxes one of the least of these commandments and teaches men so shall be called least in the kingdom of heaven, but he who does them and teaches them shall be called great in the kingdom of heaven. For I tell you, unless your righteousness exceeds that of the scribes and Pharisees, you will never enter the kingdom of heaven'?"

I: "But everything depends on the kingdom of heaven, and it's always in the future tense. I am supposed to keep these commandments and teach them so as to be great 'in the kingdom of heaven.' You want my deeds of righteousness to be more than those of the scribes and Pharisees – so that I can enter the kingdom of heaven. What about the here and now?"

He: "But don't you say the prayer I teach too: 'Our father who art in heaven, hallowed be your name. Your kingdom come, your will be done, on earth as it is in heaven.'"

I: "True, we say those same words in our prayers three times a day: '... may his kingdom rule, may his will be done ...'"

He: "So all of us Jews, all Israel, looks forward to the kingdom of heaven."

I: "True."

He: "And don't I teach that we should have trust in God and not worry about what we're going to eat or drink or wear? 'But seek first his kingdom and his righteousness, and all these things shall be ours as well. Therefore do not be anxious about tomorrow, for tomorrow will be anxious for itself. Let the day's own trouble be sufficient for the day' (Matt 6:25–34). So is the kingdom of heaven so strange to you, when your passport is trust in God?"

I: "I hear the same sentiment among the Pharisees, you know. If we can peer into the future, we'll find it in so many words." Time would prove me right; a Pharisaic master of the coming age would say the same thing in much the same words:

> Rabbi Eliezer the Great says, "Whoever has a piece of bread in his pocket and says, 'What shall I eat tomorrow?' is only one of those of little faith." That is in line with what Rabbi Eleazar said, "What is the meaning of that which is written, 'For who has despised the day of small things?' (Zech 4:10)? Who caused the table of the righteous to be despoiled in the age to come? It was the smallness [of spirit] that characterized them, for they did not believe in the Holy One, blessed be he." (Babylonian Talmud Tractate Sotah 48B)

I: "But here and now I face the choice – and you want me to choose – to follow you to Jerusalem or to stay home."

He: "True. You can come if you want."

I: "If I thought the kingdom of heaven were upon us, I'd come. But I don't, so I won't, and you do, so you're going, aren't you?"

"Yes."

"Your own words?"

"My own words."

And – for I'd missed much that he'd said – he repeated things he'd been saying here and there in Galilee, things like this:

"Go and tell John what you hear and see: the blind receive their sight and the lame walk, lepers are cleansed and the deaf hear, and the dead are raised up, and the poor have good news preached to them." (Matt 11:4–5)

"Truly I say to you, many prophets and righteous men longed to see what you see, and did not see it, and to hear what you hear, and did not hear it …" (Matt 13:17)

"For the Son of man is to come with his angels in the glory of his Father, and then he will repay every man for what he has done. Truly, I say to you, there are some standing here who will not taste death before they see the Son of man coming into his kingdom." (Matt 16:27–28)

"Lo, we have left everything and followed you. What then shall we have?"

"… in the new world, when the Son of man shall sit on his glorious throne, you who have followed me will also sit on twelve thrones, judging the twelve tribes of Israel. And everyone who has left houses or brothers or sisters or father or mother or children or lands, for my name's sake, will receive a hundredfold, and inherit eternal life." (Matt 19:27–29)

I: "It's soon."
He: "Very soon."
"But what if not?"
Long silence – a very, very long silence.
"So what will be?"
"God knows."
He arose and went his way.
I watched him walk away, till I saw his disciples coming toward him from their different paths and directions. I was sure, for now, he was all right. They would go with him to Jerusalem. They believed.

155

I didn't.

I called after him: "Go in peace – *lekh be-Shalom*."

I wished him well, but I went home.

Not disappointed, certainly not without regret – but my eyes turned homeward nonetheless. There waited my wife, my children, my dog, waiting to play with me, my plants in my garden, waiting on me to water them – my everything. There was my work, there my rest; there my calling, my task, my vocation – that vocation, and no other. Here is my *responsibility*; here is where God wants me to be: sustaining life, sanctifying life, in the here and the now of home and family, community and society. The kingdom come – indeed, but until then, my calling is in this here and now.

For with sorrow for what was to be, which I would not wish on him, I could not share his fate or join his faith, not in the crisis of death, nor (if that is what would happen) in his triumph over death. It was not that I was not persuaded in the virtue of the man, or the wisdom of some of what he said. It was that I did not hear from him the message that the Torah had told me to anticipate. His torah lacked the main thing that the Torah taught. So there was no point, even to show goodwill, to affirm all the sayings he had said that really were true to the Torah of Moses too.

The Torah had told me things about God's kingdom that Jesus neglected, and Jesus had told me things about God's kingdom that the Torah had not affirmed. Jesus' account of God's rule drew my eyes on high, to heaven. But I lived, and now live, in the here and now of goring oxen and quarreling families. The kingdom of heaven may come, perhaps not even soon enough, but until it is upon us, the Torah tells me what it means to live in God's kingdom – in the here and now.

Much that Jesus had to say about God's kingdom concerned things that the Torah, for its part, neglected too: who gets in and who doesn't, for instance. When it will be and, of course, Jesus' own situation in God's kingdom – for none of these teachings did the Torah prepare me, and in all fairness, there is no reason that it should have.

Can the kingdom of God come soon, in our day, to where we are? The Torah not only says yes, but also shows how. Indeed, that is its point. Do I have then to wait for God's kingdom? Of course I have to wait: but while waiting, there are things I have to do.

More to the point, there are things we have to do, and to do together. Jesus and his disciples went their way, off the stage of Israel's enduring life, and I would have thought then, and I think now, that Israel was right to let them take their leave. For theirs – at least in the spectacle of Matthew's picture – was a message for individuals, but the Torah spoke to us all. Leave home, follow me; give it all up, follow me; take up your (personal) cross, follow me – but then what of home, what of family and community and the social order that the Torah had commanded Israel to bring into being?

Long ago, far away, God had called a people, a holy, enduring people, into being. God had bound the people to God in a covenant, giving the Torah as terms of that agreement, engraving even into our flesh the very sign of the covenant. Nothing I heard from Jesus spoke of covenant, nothing of Israel, nothing of obligation of the whole of Israel, all together and all at once; everything spoke of me, not us; of leaving, not staying; of a near-turning, not the long-term state of affairs.

Well, I thought, what if he is right? If there is no long-term, but only this "in yet a little while ..."?

Well, he was right, wasn't he: "Do not be anxious about tomorrow, for tomorrow will be anxious for itself. Let the day's own trouble be sufficient for the day" – a message deeply rooted in the Torah that speaks of goring oxen and contentious people.

So if he's right, then the kingdom of Heaven will be here, and all the things he says will be, will be.

But if he's wrong, then what happens? Families destroyed, for what? Villages abandoned, why? And what then do we do when oxen gore and people contend?

My argument concerns not the practical as against the heavenly. It concerns two conceptions of what Heaven wants, of where Heaven must be brought to earth. The Torah has told me how to build a kingdom of priests and a holy people. So the Torah speaks of God's kingdom. But it speaks of the goring ox and the breach of trust. Real people live real lives in God's kingdom. The Torah teaches them how to build that kingdom where they are, how they are.

Nothing that Jesus has said about the kingdom of Heaven tells me that here, where we are, we can build, we can obey the Torah and so form a kingdom of priests and holy people. He speaks of Heaven, not earth; his rules are rules for his time and place, his yoke is easy and his burden is light – up there. But I walk the path down here. I go home. He calls to *me*, but I am part of *us*. He tells me to give up home and family, but God at Sinai has told us there is no kingdom of God without home and family, village and community, land and people. The kingdom of God is to come about down here, in God's people and any person may become one of God's people, Israel.

Walking home, I saw at a distance that mountain where I'd first seen Jesus, standing on the hilltop, with his disciples seated round about. Standing at the foot of the mountain, I thought of Moses on high, speaking in God's name, so long ago, but heard every day.

Yes, I'd heard "Blessed are the poor in spirit, for theirs is the kingdom of heaven; blessed are those who mourn, for they shall be comforted; blessed are the meek, for they shall inherit the earth; blessed are those who hunger and thirst for righteousness, for they shall be satisfied; blessed are the merciful, for they shall obtain mercy; blessed are the pure in heart, for they shall see God; blessed are the peacemakers, for they shall be called sons of God ..." (Matt 5:3–9).

But what had I heard from down below, where I was standing?

"The crowds were astonished at his teaching, for he taught them as one who had authority, and not as their scribes" (Matt 7:28).

Well, what about the other mountain?

"I am the Lord your God, who brought you out of the land of Egypt, out of the house of bondage.

"You shall have no other gods before me.

"You shall not make yourself a graven image … for I the Lord your God am a jealous God, visiting the iniquity of the fathers upon the children to the third and the fourth generation of those who hate me, but showing steadfast love to thousands of those who love me and keep my commandments …" (Exod 20:2–6).

Moses had said much more, standing on the mountain. He told the people how to organize their nation; how to conduct its day-to-day affairs; how to worship God and how to serve God; how God would give them a holy land and how they should farm it – everything they needed to know to build a kingdom, God's kingdom, under the rule of God through the prophet, Moses.

"And how had they responded, and how do I now respond?" – I asked myself as one mountain brought to mind the other. A sentence from the Torah came to mind:

Moses came and told the people all the words of the Lord and all the ordinances; and all the people answered with one voice, and said, "All the words which the Lord has spoken we will do." (Exod 24:3)

And there was so much more – so much more that made the mountain in Galilee seem so far from the mountain Sinai. But to say more would be to say the same thing many times over, and besides, I was near home, and as it happens, the day was Friday; the sun was setting. Jesus even then ought to have been nearing Jerusalem. I wondered what he made of the words we all would say in reciting a blessing over wine in a very few minutes:

"Wherefore the people of Israel shall keep the sabbath, observing the sabbath throughout their generations, as a perpetual covenant. It is a sign for ever between me and the people of Israel that in six days the Lord made heaven and earth, and on the seventh day he rested and was refreshed." (Exod 31:16–17)

Throughout all generations – a perpetual covenant – a sign forever: what has Sinai to do with a hill in Galilee? The covenant endures.

So he walked his way, and I mine. Really, I concluded, an argument is not all that easy when one party speaks of tomorrow, the other, today. Whether the message of that Galilean hilltop came about in that near tomorrow was not for me to say. But I knew then, and I know now, that the commanding voice of Sinai pierced the ages, and was heard, and would be heard, wherever eternal Israel endured. We would hear and obey; we do try to hear and try to obey, in God's kingdom in the here and now; the Sabbath, coming every seventh day, gives us a foretaste of the kingdom; the six days of labor – work we do together, rest we take together, we, eternal Israel, called to be, to build, the kingdom of priests and the holy people.

We do well to compete, then, and accept that judgment that is a challenge:

"Woe to you, scribes and Pharisees, hypocrites! for you traverse sea and land to make a single proselyte, and when he becomes a proselyte, you make him twice as much a child of hell as yourselves." (Matt 23:15)

And by way of our reply, we repeat what God said to us at the head of the Ten Commandments – a statement that Matthew's Jesus curiously bypasses in silence whenever he speaks of the Ten Commandments:

"I am the Lord your God, who brought you out of the land of Egypt, out of the house of bondage."

That explains what I promised to explain: why, if I had been there and been among the first to hear the this-worldly teachings – the torah with a small *t* – put forth as part of the claim in behalf of Jesus Christ, for my part, I would have dissented too. If I had heard what he said, for good and substantive reasons I would not have become one of his disciples. And for these same reasons, I am not one of his disciples today.

Can I say why in one word?

Yes, because for Jesus, "you" is as often singular as plural.

But for the Torah, from Sinai onward, "you" is always plural: "You shall have no other gods before me."

"We" – eternal Israel – are here to respond: "We shall do and we shall obey."

And I do not believe God would want it any other way.